DREAMING OF EDEN

DREAMING OF EDEN

AMERICAN RELIGION AND POLITICS IN A WIRED WORLD

Susan Brooks Thistlethwaite

palgrave
macmillan

First published in 2010 by
PALGRAVE MACMILLAN®
in the United States—a division of St. Martin's Press LLC,
175 Fifth Avenue, New York, NY 10010.

Where this book is distributed in the UK, Europe and the rest of the world,
this is by Palgrave Macmillan, a division of Macmillan Publishers Limited,
registered in England, company number 785998, of Houndmills,
Basingstoke, Hampshire RG21 6XS.

Palgrave Macmillan is the global academic imprint of the above companies
and has companies and representatives throughout the world.

Palgrave® and Macmillan® are registered trademarks in the United States,
the United Kingdom, Europe and other countries.

ISBN: 978–0–230–10780–9

Library of Congress Cataloging-in-Publication Data

Thistlethwaite, Susan Brooks, 1948–
    Dreaming of Eden : American religion and politics in a wired world /
Susan Brooks Thistlethwaite.
        p. cm.
    ISBN 978–0–230–10780–9 (hardback)
        1. Information technology—Religious aspects. 2. Information
technology—United States. 3. United States—Religion. 4. Innocence
(Theology) I. Title.

BL265.I54T45 2010
201′.66097309051—dc22   2010013777

A catalogue record of the book is available from the British Library.

Design by Newgen Imaging Systems (P) Ltd., Chennai, India.

First edition: October 2010

10 9 8 7 6 5 4 3 2 1

Printed in the United States of America.

For Rowan and Dean
because you are the future

CONTENTS

ACKNOWLEDGMENTS

Writing is not, for me, a solitary exercise and it has become even less solitary with the advent of the electronic community. Yet, I must first thank my family for being my most important community. My sons James, Bill, and Doug, my daughter-in-law, Fiona, my mother-in-law, Jeane, my sister Nancy, and especially my husband, Dick, give me love and support and challenge me intellectually. I would not have the courage to step out into cyberspace were it not for the fact that my family is always there for me, holding me in real space and time.

I also want to acknowledge the Chicago Theological Seminary for giving me a year's sabbatical, following my ten years serving as president, so that I could recover my intellectual life and write a book! I would also like to thank the Center for American Progress for making me a Senior Fellow in the Faith and Progressive Policy Initiative and for pushing me way beyond my intellectual comfort zone and challenging me to think about religion and politics in very new ways. The views expressed in this book are mine, however, and are not necessarily those of either of these fine institutions.

I owe several individuals a debt of gratitude for testing my ideas, and offering me ideas. I would like to thank Sally Steenland, Senior Policy Advisor of the Center for American Progress, for suggesting I do a blog to accompany this book. I would like to especially thank Gordon Segal, an innovative businessman, for reading the entire manuscript and pushing me hard to make a balanced case about human nature and economics. I would like to thank Howard Morgan, experienced banker and community leader, for reading the sections on banking and talking to me about real-world financial applications. Similarly, I would like to thank Connie Duckworth, a businesswoman and social entrepreneur, for catching an error in the Introduction. I would like to thank my sons not only for being supportive of my work, but also for being members of the Millennial Generation, and Generation X, and being sounding boards for me on religion and politics for their age groups. I would also like to thank Lester Feder for his insights on the wired religion of the Millennial Generation.

These days, however, the wired world adds the possibility of enormous, additional communities of engagement. I have to acknowledge the cyber community of the *Washington Post* online in the On Faith section. I deeply appreciate being asked to be a weekly contributor to the *Washington Post* online, and I need to especially thank David Waters as editor and now Elizabeth Tenety as the new editor, for being such a stimulating online dialogue partners as we considered ideas of religion and politics in this age. And I want to thank all those who post their comments on my online page; I want to thank you whether you love or hate what I write. Indeed, I learn the most from what touches a nerve in cyberspace, from what went "viral" and what just sits there, taking up lines of code and stimulating no engagement. This tells me so much about how people make meaning in a wired world. You, the cyber community, have been my greatest teachers in what I have come to call "public theology." I worked out a lot of the ideas for this book by blogging for two years and engaging with what is happening to religion in the public square in the digital age.

I want to thank the *Washington Post* online for giving me permission to use portions of those posts in this book.

I have never had an agent before for my books, and I was blessed to find Peter Rubie of FinePrint Literary Management. Peter was not only a great agent, but also a great dialogue partner about the book. He questioned me and argued with me and kept challenging me to state my ideas more and more clearly. Thanks Peter. And thank you as well to my editor at Palgrave Macmillan, Burke Gerstenschlager, who really got what I was trying to do in public theology and who is truly a theological visionary about how human beings make or break meaning in their lives and in the public square.

I also want to acknowledge the communities of people of faith, and people of humanist values, who strive every day, often against impossible odds, to make this world a more decent, healthy, peaceful, and just place. You inspire me, you give me hope and without all of you, this wired and tired old world would be a little closer to hell, and a whole lot farther from heaven.

TAKING A BIG BYTE OUT OF
A WIRED WORLD

A shiny apple with a big bite taken out of it is one of the most famous symbols in the world today. Is it the apple that Eve bit into in the Garden of Eden, and then shared with Adam? Is it the apple that got Adam and Eve kicked out of the Garden of Eden for wanting to know too much? In a way, yes it is. The shiny apple with a bite taken out of it is the symbol of Apple, Inc. and there are millions of these bitten apple symbols all around us.

Steve Jobs, one of the two founders of the company, knew exactly what he was doing when he asked his designers to come up with an apple logo with a big bite out of it. The bite symbolized the desire for new knowledge in the "bytes" of information now available to everyone through computer technology—it also symbolized the risk.[1]

Nobody has done a better job of laying out the Eden meanings in the computer age than Kurt Vonnegut. In his speech to the Syracuse University graduating class of 1994, he didn't mince words with this first Internet generation:

Now you young twerps want a new name for your generation? Probably not, you just want jobs, right? Well, the media do us all such tremendous favors when they call you Generation X, right?

Two clicks from the very end of the alphabet. I hereby declare you
Generation A, as much at the beginning of a series of astonishing
triumphs and failures as Adam and Eve were so long ago."[2]

The story of Adam and Eve and their expulsion from the innocence of the Garden of Eden may be the most famous story in
the world. It is story "A," the story of the beginning. As told in
the biblical account in Genesis, this story is humanity's attempt
to answer a fundamental question people have been asking from
ancient times until the present: "Why are things so messed up?"
The story of Adam and Eve is also a story about human desire
and the way people want to know more than they think is good for
them. This world, even with all its conflicts and violence, is very
attractive and interesting because it is so challenging. In religious
terms, we call that temptation.

The reason Steve Jobs put an apple with a bite taken out of
it on his computers is that he understands the human desire for
knowledge. to know even more than we think is good for us. But
that realization only makes us want to know more. Jobs wanted to
tempt you to knowledge when he put his bitten apple on his computers. The computer age, through the personal computer, is a
conduit to a wired world, a world with almost unlimited opportunities for good and for evil. What we need to realize about a wired
world is that the human capacity to know more good and more
evil just accelerated beyond anything people who were born 50
or 60 years ago could ever have imagined when they first became
adults.

But computers as a link to a wired world aren't just a way to get
to new knowledge; they are changing the very nature of how people learn and know things. The invention of writing was one way
that changed how people knew things. Written texts, especially

after the invention of the printing press, defined how people knew things about the world. But with the dawn of the media age in film and then television, and then the digital age with computers and the Internet, the way we know things has changed dramatically again. Writing conveys knowledge, but it a knowledge that stays on the printed page. It is also a text—it communicates more fully formed thoughts. A wired world moves and changes. It shows images more than it shows text, and the images move and change. Even words can change instantly on the Internet. Films, blogs, YouTube, Twitter, and television all convey meaning through images much more than they do text.

A wired world doesn't just change the way we receive knowledge, it changes the way we make meaning. Everybody knows that a "picture is worth a thousand words" anyway—and now we mostly get our meaning through pictures, and through pictures that are moving and changing and twinkling and blinking. Everything is speeding up and moving around. In terms of the story of the Garden of Eden, that means the kind of knowledge of good and evil that tempts us through an Apple computer, or any kind of computer, is speeding up and moving around and giving us very little time to think about it. The wired world isn't just changing how we know good and evil—in profound ways it is changing, or at least challenging, the very nature of good and evil itself. This isn't having a positive effect on us now as Americans, but that doesn't mean it couldn't have a better effect, especially if we begin to really see the possibilities of making new meanings about good and evil through the images and stories a wired world is delivering to us every day.

As Americans, we have been smack in the middle of this explosion of the Internet from the beginning. We know that a wired world delivers meaning in blinding flashes and scattered images.

It should come as no surprise, then, that Americans do not agree about 'what it all means.' As we observe our society becoming more and more polarized and inclined to fight over the meaning of both religion and politics, perhaps we ought to look at the fact that we live in a wired world now and see what impact that could be having on us, and how we can help our fractured society become a little more whole again.

A "wired world" is affecting us in a religious sense, because it is literally "tempting" us to perhaps know more than is good for us. That's why Steve Jobs was right to put a religious symbol, a bitten apple straight out of the biblical book of Genesis, on his computer.

A "wired world" is also affecting us in our politics because these images are changing how we imagine ourselves as a society, and how we make decisions not only as individuals, but also as a whole people. People who all live in the same nation compete over meaning in order to make decisions about how their society should run. We call that politics and in today's wired world, the conflicts and decisions are being played out far more in digital images and media-driven stories than ever before. The religious meaning of a wired world is found in the temptation to know more than we fear is good for us, and the political meaning of the wired world is found in the competition over the dominant images that come to define policy issues.

One thing that's not new, however, is that, for us as Americans, our religion and our politics have always gone together like ice cream and apple pie. It's uniquely American. As Americans, we have always wanted to know more, perhaps more than is good for us. And in our politics, we have always been tempted to think of ourselves as good and even innocent—a God-fearing, democratic people who are creative and dynamic. This has been a source of great strength for us as a people, but in a wired world, it is also becoming a real liability. Being tempted to think we are only innocent and good has always been risky business for humanity—but to do that in a wired world is becoming downright dangerous.

AMERICAN RELIGION AND POLITICS GO VIRAL

As stated above, American public life has always had a heaping dose of religion as part of the cultural mix. This is true even before there was a United States of America. When Christopher Columbus stumbled on to these shores, he thought he had discovered the Garden of Eden. Then the Pilgrims came, establishing the "New Jerusalem," a perfect little Eden smack dab in the middle of a frightening wilderness. The Pilgrims wanted their Jerusalem to embody social and religious perfection—what they got was conflict and dissention and immorality. In other words, what the Pilgrims got was politics.

From mythical Plymouth Rock until today, Americans continue to dream that we have created this perfect, innocent and God-fearing nation. This is the profoundly religious vision of this nation. We hold on tight to the idea of our American innocence, for better or worse. We persist in our religious vision of a perfect, God-blessed America even when that idea comes into direct conflict with the reality of our politics. As Americans we get very anxious when our religious vision of America (We're Eden! The Promised Land! God's Country!) gets too close to the realities of politics (sex scandals! death panels! jobless recovery!). That's the struggle we are in right now, as a matter of fact.

But what is genuinely new is that now this religious struggle over the meaning of America is happening in a wired world. The digital age gives enormous power both to image and storytelling, and it does so with lightening speed. Those Americans who best understand the power and the deep religious meaning of the shift to digital image and storytelling will succeed in getting their message across. That group of Americans will also understand the messages that are most dangerous to their point of view, and they will be better able to counter them. And those Americans who don't understand the religious power of this time as it is generated in blogs, movies, graphic novels, Twitter, Facebook, and cable television (to name just a few digitized sources of image and story) will be left in the dust, religiously and politically speaking.

I call this new way of thinking about religion and culture in the digital age "public theology." Public theology is often used as a term to mean relating religious doctrines to things that are happening in the public square, like "abortion is evil" or "the budget is a moral document." That is not what I mean. What I mean by Public Theology is *really seeing* the religious meaning that is being generated in the kinds of new media that pummel us all day long every day. It also means helping everybody *get* that these are major religious stories, competing stories, really, about who human beings are, what the world really is, and what people believe God is up to in the midst of all of it.

The "Reagan Revolution" in conservative politics began with Reagan's election in 1981. Jerry Falwell founded the "Moral Majority," a conservative Christian evangelical lobbying group, in 1979. Steve Jobs and Stephen Wozniak marketed the first personal computer in 1977. The thirty years of the digital age have also been the same thirty years in which America has become steadily more religiously and politically conservative. Conservative religion and politics have been far, far better than religious and political progressivism at knowing and using the power of image and storytelling to get their message across. While the successful presidential campaign of Barack Obama effectively used new technology such as Twitter and Facebook to mobilize people, especially young people, that innovation has not been extended into governance. There has been comparatively little use of digital innovation to generate support for the president's policies outside of Washington. Furthermore, what religious and political conservatives really seem to understand about our wired world is how much anxiety modern, Internet-speed culture creates. They also understand the human longing for a more innocent time, a time when there were not all these bewildering choices and images and conflicting stories. What conservatives best understand is how much Americans still long for the innocence of our founding vision, the Pilgrim vision of a perfect society, or the dream that we could get back, like Christopher Columbus dreamed, to Eden.

But still, the digital age is not necessarily either conservative or liberal in terms of religion or politics. The "wired world" has just taken the eternal human drama into cyberspace. As humans, we have always hoped we could be innocent again, and we have always feared that we are really spiraling down into chaos and despair. It is the oldest story of all. It is the story of Adam and Eve getting kicked out of the Garden of Eden. It is the story of the primal violence of Cain against Abel and the deep longing people have to return to that Garden and find innocence and safety once again. It is also the longing we have in our political life to have clear heroes and enemies, the innocent and the guilty, the guys who wear white hats and the guys who wear black hats.

Consider this startling example. The manic face of the Joker helped make the movie *The Dark Knight* into a box office smash. The manic face of the Joker digitally twisted to become the face of President Obama also became a smash hit. Starting soon after President Obama's election, it showed up on posters at political rallies protesting everything from government run health care to gun control. The political Joker image went "viral" almost overnight and it helped to change the politics of hope into the politics of fear.

The "Obama as the Joker" poster is not just politics. It is politics and religion mixed together. This particular odyssey of the Joker poser represents an eternal story of human longing for innocence, and the dangerous consequences of the power of fearing we really can't be innocent. The story of the Joker poster is about how politics itself tempts us to long for innocence, or to find our political opponents not only wrong, but demons bent on destroying us and our way of life.

Ironically enough, the image of Barack Obama as the Joker was created by a *disappointed young liberal*[3] who wanted not only political change in 2008, he wanted more dramatic change than he thought Obama represented, and he was furious that he couldn't have it. He turned his rage into a cruel parody. Firas Alkhateeb, a young Palestinian American, was just twenty when he digitally enhanced a photo of Barack Obama from a *Time Magazine* cover into the Joker character as brilliantly created by another twenty-something, the tormented actor Health Ledger. Alkhateeb seemed to be disillusioned because Obama was not *liberal enough*. He favored the ultra-liberal Dennis Kucinich.[4]

Graphic novels, films, and politics blend into a potent cultural mix in this image—a portrait of the first African American President by a disillusioned young liberal. Alkhateeb demanded not just political change from his candidate—he wanted his candidate to be the one who would instantly transform the contradictions of this world into greater liberal perfection.

And then, of course, the image was taken up by the far right, and the word "socialism" added at the bottom. That improved image perfectly fit the needs of the conservatives who also long to reestablish American innocence, (we're "free" and "democratic"), just in way diametrically opposed to the views of the image's original creator, Alkhateeb. Of course, the "socialism" label really meant "fear," and the enhanced image went viral.

The extraordinary polarization of American politics today comes from competing and contradictory religious stories about who people really are and whether change is really possible, digitally enhanced and moving at the speed of light. These are stories of sin and salvation, of innocence and guilt, and they are being played out right there in front of us in the ordinary stuff of our new culture. We see it on posters at rallies, in films and graphic novels, on the radio and in blogs, and of course, on cable television.

And every day this speeds up. If anything, the political climate in the United States has become more virulently polarized since the new President took office, not less. More and more, the country is starting to resemble the 1960s when the politics of anger, invented (and some would say perfected) by Richard Nixon,[5] hopelessly divided the country. Conservatives are stoking the smoldering resentments of middle America, resentments re-ignited by the economic downturn. Liberals dream that if only "extremists" would just quit and "see *reason*" all would be well.[6] But it's all happening in images projected throughout cyberspace, and this makes these issues more urgent and dangerous than ever before in human history.

WHY IT IS DANGEROUS TO
DREAM OF EDEN NOW

The lessons of the Garden of Eden have never been timelier. Humans are already prone to fear and anxiety and a wired world makes this tendency more extreme. Even under the best of circumstances, people aren't always reasonable; they are creative *and* chaotic, productive *and* destructive. The one thing people are not is *innocent*.

It's also good not to fall prey to the tempting extremes of digitally enhanced culture. We dare not be either too optimistic, or too pessimistic about human nature. Yes, people aren't innocent, but that doesn't mean that they're no good either. Most people and societies are a complicated mix of both.

If we're going to engage people as they really are, not as we would wish them to be, we need to take seriously that human beings are excellent at lying to themselves, and they tend to believe what they want to believe. But people are also very creative and they do make adaptive changes all the time that can improve their own lives and the lives of others. So we have to tell meaningful stories and lift up powerful images that catch people in their subconscious first, where all the really big decisions are made. We live by stories, big images of who we are and how the world works.

It is truly surprising how many of the stories in popular culture are actually Garden of Eden stories. Many of them tempt us to believe we are innocent in one way or another. Some of the stories tell us we are guilty and drive us to despair. Other stories let us into the contradictions of human nature, while still giving us the capacity to engage the very human wisdom that has gotten us this far. This kind of wisdom is far from naïve—it's 'knowing good and evil' as the serpent says in Genesis.

In short, we need to find the stories of the Garden of Eden that show us we cannot get back to innocence and *that's not necessarily a bad thing*. We can read the Garden of Eden as a story of human experimentation and risk, not just sin and damnation. Retelling the story of human nature, about its strengths and weaknesses, can help us understand human beings more deeply so that we can stimulate human creativity and rein in the worst of human destructive tendencies. Deep change, however, takes a very long time, and really positive change for this country will not come without a change in the deep scripts we live by, not just change in policies and programs. Americans who want real change must give up their dreams of innocence and the idea that if you just tell people to be good, they'll be good. God tried that in the Garden of Eden and it didn't work out. Why?

People are still trying to figure that out. That's why Garden of Eden stories are all around us, especially now in the digital age. People have always wondered why, despite our best efforts to lead decent lives, we keep messing up, and there are many stories about how and why that happens, and what we have to do to fix it. Popular culture is more and more becoming a powerful way these stories get told and retold in different ways that influence our political behavior. Popular culture is ever more accessible in the digital age, not just to users, but also to creators. That's part of the story of the Garden of Eden too, that after we get kicked out of the Garden of Eden, human beings are both creative and destructive.

PUBLIC THEOLOGY

I call this approach public theology, which represents a new method for thinking about religion *and* the public square. Public theology shows how popular culture tells and retells religious stories, like the Garden of Eden story, in different ways and with different outcomes. People use popular culture to make religious meaning. In movies, on television, in YouTube videos, blogs, comics, and in songs we are telling each other stories all day long. Americans make meaning through these cultural creations, and we challenge one another's meaning through them as well. It's also the way we shape and re-shape our politics.

This is the way the deep meaning of our lives is actually debated. Seminary professors and many pastors may think people actually know or care a lot about religious doctrine. Most people, however, neither understand doctrines, nor do they care about them. What they care about is making some meaningful sense of their lives and the world around them. Is it Wall Street greed, or the threats of 'socialism' that are to blame for our declining economy? Is government the problem, or the solution?

I have to hand it to the Christian conservatives, and especially the mega-church pastors. They truly understand that people want to make sense of their lives much more than they want to know about the doctrine of the Trinity. Christian conservatives are the religious leaders who talk directly to the American people about religion and values and they make the case that their view of the world is the right one. They recognize, like Rick Warren, that people want to live a *Purpose Driven Life*. Warren doesn't use technical, religious vocabulary in his books or sermons, but talks simply and easily about people's everyday lives, society, our world, and the religious meaning of it all.

I just happen to disagree profoundly with Warren's perspective, and indeed I think his views, along with those of other conservatives, have helped drive this country into a ditch. But it is not wise to ignore what Warren or T. D. Jakes or Joel Hunter do—they make their case to people in general language and using the stuff of people's lives to pitch their religious argument.

For the last several years, I too have been trying to talk directly to the American people about why we need a different religious perspective on the big issues of our time. I have been writing weekly posts for the *Washington Post*'s "On Faith" blog. More and more I have worked out a way to talk about a religious view of the economy, of international relations, politics, and a host of public issues using images from popular culture. In fact, I got the idea for this book because I get so many posts to the blog that ask me to go farther with my observations. Why is the new *Star Trek* movie helpful in getting people to think that it's possible to avoid a nuclear holocaust? Why do other culturally powerfully narratives, like the *Left Behind* series of novels, help lay the religious groundwork for attacking Iraq? I wrote about that as *Armageddon Tired of This War*. The *Left Behind* novels give people the big idea that the world is about to end. That's the Christian doctrine called Armageddon. But the *Left Behind* novels make that hoary old theology of the end of the world sound like it's going to be fun for some, and payback for others.

The very future of our planet, our lives, and our children's lives are at stake in these real culture wars. The real culture wars are wars of images and stories, not just struggles over particular policies like abortion or gay rights. Those kinds of cultural struggles are the foreground, but the real war will be won or lost in the background, in the war of competing stories and images. We need to know that and make sure everybody knows that by promoting creative cultural images and scripts we can actually solve the real problems we face, not just blow up the planet and start over in heaven.

That is why, in addition to this book that sets out my views on human nature, popular culture, and public policy, I have created the blog www.wiredwisdom.net. On a daily basis, the way in which the myths of American innocence collide with fights in the public square about policy shift rapidly. This book sets out the idea that we live in the public square according to deep cultural scripts. The blog is about up-to-the minute struggles where, if we dream of innocence, we will literally lose a policy debate. And if we are better at changing the big story and challenging conservative control of the meaning of the story, and their preferred narrative, we will finally get to a more progressive American reality in terms of public policy.

Our only choices are *not* just between an unrealistic hope, and a fear and loathing of each other. If we're going to find those choices, we need to find better images and public theological narratives that can bring the hope down to earth, and turn the fear into passion for what we can achieve. But if we insist on longing for the innocence of Eden, either on the right or the left, the forces at play in the twenty-first century will literally sweep over us like the increasingly powerful tsunamis produced by global climate change. And we will drown in our own fears and disappointed hopes.

OVERVIEW

The first part of this book, titled "Dreaming of Eden" consists of two chapters. Chapter 1, "Adam, Eve, and the Garden of Eden" retells the story of Adam and Eve and the Garden of Eden through two films that have been very popular in the last two decades. One is a conservative story of the "fall" and redemption, the other is a liberal story about Adam and Eve and the new knowledge they gain when they lose their innocence. Chapter 2, "Citizens Cain and Abel" continues the retelling of the Genesis story about what happens after innocence. Living after the fall from innocence is hard for humanity, and the more complex society becomes, the more difficult it becomes. "Power," especially the kind of power used in war, can be a really tempting way to try to solve the problem of modern life and the thirst for innocence. This chapter concludes with the enormous complications for human nature introduced by the digital age.

In the second part, "The Danger of Innocence," there are three chapters outlining in more detail exactly how dangerous innocence has become in modern life and why the conservative Christian invitation to return to innocence is so tempting to America. One chapter is about how we got to the attack on Iraq and the policy of torture. The second is about how ideas of the "innocence" of the markets led us to deregulate them and then find ourselves with an economic meltdown. The third chapter is about how both evangelicals and some environmental liberals both dream of innocence and a return to Eden as a way to deal with climate change. Of course, each group has a very different view of the Eden to which they want to return!

In the third part, "A Better Story," I show how being good is not the same thing as being innocent. We can have a workable approach to national security and a productive economy without big booms followed by big busts. We can be "green" without being romantic—this is a lesson we can learn from the "twenty-something" generation who are both idealistic and less innocent than their parents and grandparents.

In conclusion, I gather some examples of "wired wisdom" to tell a new story about the Garden of Eden through the tendrils of creativity that persist in springing up in our chaotic digital age. Kurt Vonnegut is right; this is the beginning of human history all over again.

PART ONE

Dreaming of Eden

ONE

ADAM, EVE, AND
THE GARDEN

(4 ne)

Reinhold Niebuhr, perhaps the most famous American theologian of the twentieth century, was once asked if he thought the story of Adam and Eve in the Garden of Eden is "literally true." "No," replied Niebuhr seriously, "it's truer than that." What Niebuhr meant was that if the story of Adam and Eve is reduced to an argument about who was wearing fig leaves and when, the truth of the story is missed. The deeper truth found in the story of Adam and Eve concerns a loss of innocence. We are "fallen," which means that we can be tempted and we sometimes do things we know we shouldn't do. That's the human condition in a nutshell. Sometimes, we sin.

The story of Adam and Eve has been interpreted time and again, even very recently, to encourage us to view our lives in certain ways. The different interpretations have huge consequences. Are there a few "saved" individuals who deserve to be rich, and others are damned, deserving of poverty and a lack of basic human rights? Did Jesus come to declare war on the sinful people, or to teach us to love one another? Is human life simply a battleground between the saved and the damned, the good and the evil, those who deserve to be rich and those who deserve to be poor? Or is human life a shared experience of the struggle to be decent in a world of conflicting good, as well as conflicting evil? When it comes to the story of Adam and Eve and the fall from innocence in the Garden of Eden, the devil really *is* in the details. The same story can be told in very different ways and thus lead individuals and whole societies to make different choices about what they think is right or wrong, moral or immoral, good or evil.

THE PUBLIC THEOLOGY OF HOLLYWOOD

Running through our public lives are stories—deep scripts that tell us who we are as individuals and as a society. These stories are essentially religious because they are about ultimate meaning and purpose. That is how the great Protestant theologian Paul Tillich actually defined religion: he said it is "ultimate concern." Each religion has its own version of ultimate concern, but all share a concern for meaning.

Our ultimate concern is especially visible at times of national crises such as domestic unrest regarding race, economic problems, or foreign wars. Particularly in times of distress, people often want to "go back to their roots," and as has been noted, the story of Adam and Eve and the Garden of Eden is one of the root stories of humanity; it is story "A." In recent years, Hollywood has provided us with two very distinct scripts about the story of Adam and Eve, the "fall" from the innocence of the Garden of Eden, and what that actually means for people living today. These two very different versions of the story reveal some of the deep roots of political conflicts among Americans right now, and also suggest clues about how to address those conflicts in more creative ways.

SCRIPT ONE: THE GARDEN OF EDEN AS BATTLEGROUND

In 2002, Mel Gibson produced and directed a reinterpretation of Jesus' death and resurrection for our turbulent times. It's titled *The Passion of the Christ*. I refer to it as "Mel Makes a War Movie"[1] because the film is constructed in such a way that the main drama is a declaration of war on sin. The movie contains only thirty seconds on Jesus' life and his teaching. The rest is a very violent interpretation of his death and resurrection.

The Passion of the Christ looks like it is a movie about Jesus' suffering and death. But it is really a Garden of Eden story. In *The Passion of the Christ*, the character of Jesus is presented as the "new Adam" who doesn't give in to the snake. In the original Garden of Eden story, Adam messes up by giving in to the temptation represented by his wife giving him the forbidden fruit of the tree of the knowledge of good and evil. In the original, Adam takes the bait of the devil, in the form of the snake, and he falls from innocence. But in *The Passion of the Christ,* Jesus of Nazareth doesn't give in to temptation. He does the Garden of Eden right for a change. In practical, political terms, what this can mean is that true believers, the followers of Jesus, can also "do the Garden of Eden right" and become innocent again by being "Christ-like." The extreme self-righteousness of 'Christian politics' has its origins in this version of the Garden of Eden story.

While many Hollywood films play to the mythic dimensions of good vs. evil, we don't often see the devil personified as in the first scene of *The Passion of the Christ,* where the devil appears to Jesus as he is praying in the Garden of Gethsemane. As the film opens, a handheld camera leads the viewer, evoking a nausea inducing, destabilizing feeling reminiscent of *The Blair*

Witch Project. It reminds the viewer of a documentary, and gives a sense that 'you are there.' The Garden of Gethsemane is depicted as a smoke-filled, primeval forest, rather than a garden, and the viewer knows nothing good is going to happen in this garden.

Jesus appears, agonizing in prayer. A black-cowled figure looms in front of the prostrate Jesus. The eyebrowless face under the cowl is pale white, feminized rather than explicitly feminine (though Mel Gibson did use the pronoun "she" in the Diane Sawyer interview, only to then, when sharply questioned by Sawyer, add "he, it"). The horror quality of the film is enhanced when a maggot comes out of the figure's nose.

The camera slowly pans down the devil's black, slimy robe, and a snake slithers to the ground out from under the robe. Now we know we are not really in the Garden of Gethsemane; we are visually in the Garden of Eden. In Eden, evil comes from the female and it comes in the form of a snake. The snake crawls menacingly toward the prostrate, seemingly helpless praying Jesus, and then the snake rears as if to strike.

Jesus jumps up and stomps the snake to death, as in the story of the cursing of the snake from Genesis 3:15. In Genesis, as a result of the snake's role in tempting the woman to eat the fruit from the tree of knowledge, God condemns the snake to "enmity" with humankind, and says people will strike the snake on the head. In his movie, Mel Gibson brings the "fall" from the Garden of Eden into the New Testament. As we know, neither Satan nor a snake appear in any New Testament accounts of Jesus in Gethsemane. Gibson is establishing the idea that Christianity is about the fact that Jesus came to defeat sin, the sin that happened because of Adam and Eve listening to the snake and then disobeying God in the Garden of Eden.

No one who has reviewed this film, whether positively or negatively, fails to mention the extraordinary amount of violence. Violence in the movies is nothing new. Hollywood has had a love affair with violence from the time of silent films. From *Birth of a Nation* to *Natural Born Killers,* it is clear that violence sells. But there are artistic as well as commercial reasons for violence in a movie. The violence in the Gibson film appears to serve another purpose; not just to sell tickets or display artistic story telling. The result of all the violence on a lot of moviegoers was to make them feel very, very guilty. During the unrelenting carnage of the flogging of Jesus, a scene that drags on, beginning to end, for forty minutes, the mind finally shuts down in defense as the emotional grief overwhelms. The extreme violence of the film is by design. The design is to keep the viewer so shocked he or she won't be able to think clearly about whether this is really the Christian story or not. The viewer becomes filled with shame and guilt and a strong desire for repentance. This is the goal of the film, to emotionally *convict* the viewer and establish that people are sinful and deserve to be punished, punishment that Jesus took in our stead. The Christian story of the "good news" that Jesus forgives our sins instead becomes a story of "bad news" about why the human desire to know good and evil is the source of our everlasting guilt for our role in causing Jesus to suffer such horrible torture.

The last scene in *The Passion of the Christ* is the most revealing. The camera focuses on a shroud fluttering down onto an empty slab in a tomb. Jesus, now healed from the savage beating he received, sits up. Drums pound, drums very like the drums of one of Gibson's other heroic war films, *Braveheart.* and Jesus looks very angry. He stomps out of the tomb, clearly bent on waging further war on sin. The message is this: 'Sinners, watch out!'

The Gibson film may have had a highly religious theme, but it had huge political and social intentions as well. This is not new. From Paul's letters in the New Testament to the early Church "fathers," through the Middle Ages, the Reformation, and right up to the present, religion and politics have worked together. For Paul, Jesus rose in order to make things right between God and humanity; things had gone horribly wrong in the Garden of Eden, and Jesus, as the "new Adam" is the one to make it right again. Remember at the time of Paul, Christians were a persecuted minority and not especially interested in the worldly, political power of the Roman Empire.

During the Middle Ages all that changed. In that period, Christianity became the official religion of the empire. Politics and religious views reinforced each other. The idea of Jesus' suffering—more than his resurrection—helped reinforce the power of the King and make the King seem more like God. This idea, called "substitutionary atonement" because Jesus "subs" for humanity, has been referred to as "the most unfortunately successful idea in the history of Christian thought" (John Dominic Crossan). It is unfortunate because the rank and file of Christians then are persuaded they deserve a whole lot of punishment and protesting their suffering at the hands of unjust political and religious rulers is not only wrong, it's evil because they deserve to suffer.[2] It's a powerful method of exercising social control.

During the Age of Enlightenment in Euro-Atlantic culture, democratic ideals of inalienable human rights supplanted the absolute power and authority of the King. Religion and democracy also worked together, and liberal theology was invented. Liberal theologies stressed Jesus' life and teaching, rather than his suffering and death, and they corresponded well with the rationalist views that gave birth to democracy.

However, in the last twenty-five years in the United States, we have experienced a backlash against democracy and its freedoms. There has been an effort on the part of religious and political conservatives to exercise "dominion" over political life.[3] The idea that God is a King who is owed a big bloody sacrifice has come back into American religion in a far more central way because God as King is a top-down model of a ruler, and reinforces a top-down kind of politics. Thomas Jefferson and other founding fathers of American democracy, by contrast, saw God as the one who created humanity with "inalienable" rights, including freedom from political and religious tyranny, and their religious views gave rise to an understanding of American political power as invested in the people. Democracy is a "bottom-up" understanding of power; those who want to change American democracy into a "top-down" notion of power love the idea of God as a tyrannical King who demands bloody sacrifices. Political tyranny goes hand-in-hand with divine tyranny; democracy requires a divine-human partnership as its religious model.

For the millions of Americans who saw Gibson's film, the message was not only that sinners better watch out, but that only such a big, bloody sacrifice as Jesus made through his intense suffering was enough to restore the innocence of the Garden of Eden to those who believe. But this innocence is not, shall we say, *innocent* in the way it is presented in the film. Who could rejoice in an innocence restored at such a price? This can be compared to letting your beloved brother be tortured so you won't be punished for something you actually did. So while you are led to believe that you have been saved by the fact that Jesus took your sins on himself and paid for them by enduring torture and a horrible death, you also end up feeling really guilty about it because it was so horrible and you really didn't deserve to have Jesus suffer this much for you because in truth you are not worthy of it. This is an unholy and unstable mixture of innocence and guilt, hope and anger. An innocence purchased at such a price, I would think, must be defended at all costs because it is so richly undeserved. People are prone to protest their innocence far more vigorously when they really fear, deep down in their hearts, they are not all that innocent and they are getting a break they don't really deserve.

SCRIPT TWO: ADAM AND EVE GET CREATIVE

A very different and innovative approach to thinking about the guilt or innocence of human beings can be found in another script: the 1998 movie, *Pleasantville*. This film was nominated for an Academy Award and takes the approach that everything interesting and creative, including failure and loss, happens after Adam and Eve mess up and get thrown out of the Garden of Eden.

In the film *Pleasantville*, the meaning of the story of Adam and Eve, the snake, and the Garden is less like the punishing version in Mel Gibson's *The Passion of the Christ*, and more like the view of Irenaeus of Lyon, a third century Christian theologian. Irenaeus thought that the fall was "upward," and argued that people were not created as perfect and then became imperfect through the fall; people were naïve when they were created and over time had to learn. Temptation by the devil was a good thing, because it started humanity on a journey toward knowledge, though it is risky and many things can and will go wrong.

In the movie *Pleasantville*, the role of the devil is played by a TV repairman (Don Knotts). The plot revolves around teenage twins, David and Jennifer, who are as different as night and day. The brother, David, is a couch potato who spends all day watching reruns of an old black-and-white sitcom called *Pleasantville*, while trying to tune out his unhappy single mother. His sister, Jennifer, is one of the popular kids, obsessed with her appearance and her social life.

When the TV remote gets broken during an argument, a strange TV repairman shows up and gives David a special remote that teleports both siblings to the world of Pleasantville where everything is seemingly perfect. The basketball team has never lost a game, it has never rained, there have been no fires, no one ever gets angry, and everything is pleasant. All of this takes place in black and white. It is 1950s America reminiscent of *Leave It to Beaver* and *Father Knows Best*. And it is incredibly boring. David and Jennifer, in their characters as Bud and Mary Sue Parker, start asking questions and not following the regular plot of the sitcom. While at Lover's Lane, Jennifer introduces Skip Martin, the basketball champion, to sex and he tells the whole team about it. The team loses their next game and the community is shocked.

All this new knowledge causes a tree to burst into flames. David (as Bud) recognizes that it's a fire and rushes to get the firemen. The firemen have no idea what to do, never having had to put out a fire; David shows them how to use the hose. Then David explains how he knows about fire and how there is a wider world beyond Pleasantville. When he summarizes the plot of *Huckleberry Finn*, the formerly blank pages of the book fill in with words, and suddenly the whole town is rushing to the library to get books.

With this new knowledge, the world of Pleasantville begins to show some color. Some people gain color from having sex, some from reading books, and others from experiencing strong feelings of love or anger. When Bud and the owner of the local corner store paint one side of city hall with brilliant colors, they are arrested and put on trial. The trial was a sham because they don't know why they are being charged, and are not given legal counsel. They are told that they can't have a lawyer in order to "keep everything pleasant." The citizens who have turned from black and white to color have to sit in the balcony in the courthouse. Those who are still black and white sit in the lower seating.

David's defense is to tell those assembled that it's okay if everything isn't perfect. When the mayor becomes outraged, he turns to color and then a citizen tells everyone the whole town is in color. The film ends with three of the main characters, residents of Pleasantville, sitting on a bench and admitting that they don't know what will happen next.

All the elements of the story of the "fall" are present in this film, the desire for new knowledge, including sexual knowledge, and the inevitable problems that come about when you know too much, but they are placed in a very different context and thus the conclusions we draw from the fact that people do "mess up" end up being very different. *The Passion of the Christ* tells the story of sin and salvation in terms of justifying torture and faith as war on the devil. *Pleasantville* tells the story of sin and salvation in terms of the struggles for racial equality in recent American history.

The black-and-white setting of *Pleasantville* evokes an image of the 1950s and its surface conformity. When color contrast is introduced through the Civil Rights movement, this can appear to be the destruction of a "nice" and predictable way of life, but in reality it is a "fall upward" toward a more complex and interesting society. In *Passion,* the devil is pure evil and must be defeated (killed). In *Pleasantville,* the devil is the one who tempts us to know more than many would think is good for us. The TV repairman, who plays the role of the devil, isn't evil in himself. He provides a way for Bud and Mary Sue to know more about the world, and about themselves, if they choose to. Some of what they learn is hard, even painful, but it isn't necessarily wrong. In the *Pleasantville* Garden of Eden, knowledge of good and evil does introduce conflict, pain, suffering, and loss, but it also enables creativity, variety, and cultural transformation.

AMERICANS ARE LESS INNOCENT

The popular image of American life after the 1960s is no longer innocent. The struggles of the last decades are now termed "culture wars" or "politics of anger" but they are actually struggles between black-and-white certainty and dynamic color contrasts. These are struggles between innocence and knowledge, between a willed certainty and a recognition of the deeply textured nature of truth.

Like the expulsion from the Garden of Eden, the legacy of the 1960s may finally be the way this nation comes to a deeper knowledge of good and evil in both individual and communal life. We have to live in uncertainty in order to have texture, color, and creativity in our lives. Life comes with no guarantees, including no guarantees of success.

Pleasantville as a film is the product of a more liberal era, the 1990s. During the Clinton years, women's access to reproductive services increased, gay rights became a serious civil rights issue, and intensive efforts were undertaken to negotiate peace in the Middle East. While these efforts did lead to conservative backlash, they also exposed ways in which conflicts at home and abroad were hidden from view. The really imaginative point of the plot of *Pleasantville* is that perfect human relations, such as we imagine to be the case in the "Garden of Eden," are artificial and hide conflicts that really do exist. Surface conformity creates a society that is not only repressive, it's boring and without the kinds of conflicts that make human life textured and interesting. It's also clear from the film that when they are pushed, the nice folks of Pleasantville can be nasty and even violent. The pleasant façade of the innocent Garden of Eden is just that, a façade. It hides a lot of sins and is riddled with hypocrisy.

The turning point of the film is the acquisition of new knowledge. The empty pages of the library books fill with words, telling forbidden stories. This is where the liberal bent of the film, that if people only know good they will be good, needs some additional realism. There is real risk in telling the story of Adam and Eve as a story of human trial and error, and learning from their mistakes. People do learn from their mistakes, it's true, and in that way we do fall "upward." But human beings have this incredible capacity as well to *refuse to learn from their mistakes*. Human history has not been a smooth journey of learning from our mistakes and improving our lives. People are continually tempted by money, power, sex and have to make choices about what is right and wrong.

In addition, people don't fall into these traps all by themselves. We make a mistake in thinking about human nature if we put too much emphasis on the individual either in the conservative or the liberal view. Conservative religion focuses on the individual as sinner (and then on some individuals as saved), the liberal view focuses on individuals as rational and able to know the good and choose the good.

The *Pleasantville* script avoids the trap of just focusing on individuals. The film portrays two societies, the boring and limited black and white one, and the complex, challenging one in 'living color.' People in the social structure of the boring black and white, "perfect" society become different as their social relations change and they become more dynamic and interesting. What is missing, of course, is all the struggle of the Civil Rights movement that came in between. This is where the thinking on human nature has changed in the fifty or so years since Reinhold Niebuhr wrote.

In the thinking of Niebuhr, and the fourth century saint who influenced him so much, Augustine of Hippo, the root of sin is in the individual's will. It's people who mess up. They do what they don't want to do, and they don't do what they know they should do (to paraphrase a frustrated Apostle Paul).

Niebuhr (and other "Christian realists") gave much more attention than earlier thinkers to the way in which sinful human choices negatively affected societies, like creating unjust economic systems or political systems that crushed individual freedoms. But they viewed these social problems as collections of individuals making bad and worse choices. The new way of looking at the "fall" from the Garden of Eden is that people struggle together with the consequences of their actions, and these have both individual and social effects. Even Cain and Abel, as we'll see in the next chapter, have some things already set up for them, like their different jobs and the way in which those jobs may have influenced their behaviors.

When you're born, you become part of an established class, race, nation, family, and society. All of these things are part of your reality. You grow up surrounded with money or the lack of it, great education or substandard education, two parents, one parent, or no parents, and so on. Some of the things that surround you are the result of other peoples' sin and greed and narrow-mindedness, like crumbling schools with poor teachers, racist attitudes that make you feel like an outsider in your own country, and dirty, substandard housing built with cheap materials that

gives you asthma. Other things in your surroundings are products of positive efforts. For instance, here in Chicago where I live,
all the public parks bordering Lake Michigan, which are open to
all citizens for their enjoyment, are the result of other people's
collected goodness. Many good people of Chicago fought for the
lakefront to be open to the public rather than private property.
They fought hard so that all the people who live in the city could
have some breathing room.

Things like decent city planning, or substandard housing are
like cards you are dealt when you are born, except the dealer isn't
playing with a completely honest deck. Some of the cards in the
deck are bad ones, like having to live in substandard housing,
and some are good ones like getting to live in a city or town that
is well-planned, has open spaces and even decent air quality. The
good and bad cards come from good and bad choices other people have made, but you have to live with those choices in your
own life. It's true that individual initiative can count. Different
people can play with approximately the same cards and have different outcomes through individual initiative or just plain luck.
The idea that you can always overcome the obstacles of getting
dealt a bad hand in life by hard work, what's often called "pull-
yourself-up-by-your-own-bootstraps" philosophy, is overrated;
people who achieve against the odds usually have had plenty of
help and a lot of good luck along the way, And you and I in turn
make choices both in our individual lives and in the kind of society we strive to make with others that in turn affect the chances
of generations to come.

Thinking about how all of our good and bad choices affect not
just us, but our whole society helps us make some important connections. First, we can see that a lot of the inequalities into which
people are born are not necessarily natural, just there like gravity.

A lot of the time, some people helped create those inequalities. The really good news, however, is that what some people created, other people can change. We now know that racism, for example, isn't forever; it can be confronted and its legal and its cultural effects can be changed. We know that for sure because the United States elected Barack Obama, a man of mixed racial heritage, including African heritage, as president. That one vote didn't fix everything, but it sure sent a signal that attitudes on race can be changed. In fact, we know this because in discussing the obvious racially motivated backlash against President Obama's initiatives, many centrists and those on the right go to great lengths to protest that signs showing Obama as Hitler at rallies, for example, "aren't racist, it's about policy." They say that because at some level many Americans now acknowledge that racism is *wrong*. That doesn't stop these same Americans from being racist, but it is a modest indication that people know that it's not okay to be racist.

Second, we actually know that we can work together to resist all the collected sin that has piled up in our societies and our world. We can resist individually, of course, and we can work with others in social movements. All the social and individual goodness that has gone before, like the accumulated sin, is also part of our present.

For example, my grandparents, and great aunts and uncles emigrated from Hungary in the early part of the twentieth century. As children, they worked in sweatshops in the garment district of New York City and suffered life-long illnesses from working in those conditions. My great aunt joined the International Ladies Garment Workers Union and helped organize for better working conditions. The ILGWU was central in achieving the 40-hour workweek, and especially in agitating for workplace safety. After the Triangle Shirtwaist Factory fire, in 1911, in which more than

123 young women, and 23 young men died, unionization increased, especially through the 1930s, and conditions improved.[4] As a whole society, we outlawed child labor (though we have not succeeded in completely getting rid of it in, for example, farm work) and that has helped the lives of other children in this country. Other countries around the world are in similar struggles for better working conditions.

But if the good news is that people can make positive changes and reduce social inequalities, the bad news is that what some people changed for the good, other people can wreck.[5] The gains of one generation in creating better social conditions can be lost in another generation. In fact that's happening today to American workers through globalization. Now American workers compete with workers in countries that have not had labor movements and who have very or no protections for their workers, and child labor is rampant. It is critical that we see such global conditions not merely as the inevitable consequences of a globalizing economy, but also as systems of sin that need a comprehensive, not just an individualistic solution. The good of globalization, including cheaper goods available to more people, should not be allowed to obscure the cost to human economic security as whole industries change overnight, leaving their workers behind.

Knowing that all the good and all the sins are connected and on the move is a good thing. It is not only the loss of innocence, it is the beginning of wisdom.

TWO

CITIZENS CAIN AND ABEL

I t's difficult to accept idea that the "fall" from innocence was not a bad thing. The idea that good and evil are related and are intertwined in a complicated dance is disturbing and challenging. We long to believe that complete innocence is possible and that to be innocent is a wholly good thing. More "innocent" times in human history are remembered romantically, whether in a perfect garden as in Genesis, or in 1950s America.

People want to believe innocence is at least possible, even in politics, though there is repeated evidence there is no chance our politicians (or entertainers or bankers or anyone else) are wholly innocent. Claims of innocence are based on the idea that it's possible for people to *be* wholly innocent. In public and private life, however, no one is ever wholly innocent. This is the deep truth behind the biblical stories of Adam and Eve, and their first children, Cain and Abel. People aren't angels.

But the story is even more complex than that, because the conflicts in our nature are also the source of our creativity and our drive. Human beings have evolved beyond the hunter gatherer stage. Humans have settled down, invented agriculture, built cities and formed civilizations. We kept inventing new ways of farming, making goods, and delivering services. We studied the earth and the heavens, found cures for disease, and eventually left the earth in rockets to explore space. We wired the world so that information can move at lightening fast speed. And along the way, we also invented war, genocide, the atomic bomb, which could end all life on earth. We caused famines from carelessly over planting our soil; and some of us enslaved others out of greed and cruelty. And now our wired world is not only changing how our knowledge of ourselves and others is delivered, it may be changing the nature of knowledge itself. Human beings are not innocent, not at all, but we are very creative and interesting. It starts to get interesting with Cain and Abel.

CAIN AND ABEL

The story of Cain and Abel is quite old and appears in Christianity, Judaism, and Islam. The stories are very similar, but with key differences. Cain is the older brother and a farmer; his younger brother, Abel, is a shepherd. Both of them make sacrifices to God. God accepts Abel's sacrifice, but not Cain's. Cain kills Abel (Genesis 4:1-16; Qur'an at 5:26-32). The oldest version of the story we have in a written form is found in the Dead Sea Scrolls and dates from the mid first century CE, or Common Era.

In the Qu'ran, after Cain's deed is discovered by God, Cain repents. In the Genesis version, there is a slightly different take. After God discovers that Cain has murdered Abel, God banishes him, and Cain is distraught. As an outcast, he fears that everyone will try to kill him. God puts a mark on him so that everyone will know that to kill Cain will bring down God's vengeance "seven-fold." Cain goes away to the land of Nod, "east of Eden," marries, has a son, Enoch, and founds a city that he names after his son.

The story of Cain and Abel has been interpreted for thousands of years. It has been especially compelling for Christians. New

Testament writers drew parallels between the killing of innocent Abel and the crucifixion of the innocent Jesus, though the shedding of Jesus' blood saves, whereas Abel's blood does not (see Matthew 23:35 and Hebrews 12:24). In Christian history, Abel is often a stand-in for the innocent suffering of Jesus, and/or the Christian martyrs. In Christian art, especially in the Middle Ages, Cain is depicted as a stereotypical Jew, with beard and curls and even red hair—often shown killing a blond, European-looking Abel. This served to fuel anti-Semitism for centuries.

Cain has also been a stand-in for Satan and the theme of evil. According to Mormon tradition, it was Satan who tempted Cain to present the offering that was rejected, thus starting the whole fatal drama. Cain himself is used as a figure to represent evil in human nature. Cain is the biblical figure for the origin of human violence.

The primal violence in the first family has been a major artistic theme, from carvings on Medieval Cathedrals to paintings, stories, novels, and poems. John Steinbeck's magnum opus, *East of Eden*, comes as close as any work to capturing the awful biblical themes of the fundamental disorder in the human condition that Cain and Abel represent, and especially the problems of human freedom and human guilt.

Critics originally did not like the book, but it became a best seller almost immediately. There have been films, television series, and an opera based on the novel. A Korean television series based on *East of Eden* began in August 2008 and is extremely popular. *East of Eden* has even penetrated American pop culture. In one episode of the TV series *Family Guy*, Brian (the family dog) mercilessly ribs the youngest son, Stewie, for reading *East of Eden* in the car. The dog insists Stewie is only reading it because it was featured on *Oprah's Book Club*. Finally Stewie concedes the point.

Oprah Winfrey knows very well that people are drawn to literature that delves into the problems people face in their families. The problem of resentment, sibling rivalry, and even family violence are big themes in the Cain and Abel story. But what most people don't realize is that Cain and Abel is also a political story. For example, the "Mark of Cain" was interpreted by pro-slavery advocates as black skin and used to justify enslaving people of African descent, even though that's a complete misreading of Genesis. These foundational stories, such as Adam and Eve, or Cain and Abel, can take on a life of their own in culture and in history, and in the telling and re-telling emphasize completely opposite meanings of the original story.

While Cain's story has been used for practical, political ends, it is also possible to see that the story of Cain and Abel is about the fact that human civilization as a whole comes about because of an act of violence. Cain murders Abel, becomes a wanderer and then the Bible credits him with *inventing civilization.* An aspect of the story of Cain that is almost always overlooked is that the Bible credits Cain with being the first recorded person to found a city. While his father Adam had the job of naming the animals, Cain founds a city and then names it Enoch after his son. This is humanity's first established place outside the Garden of Eden and it is not wholly evil, just because it was established by Cain, but neither is it entirely innocent. The fact that the first city is founded by a murderer is a testimony to how conflicted human beings are about their own creativity—the seeds of violence seem to lurk, even in the higher achievements of culture.

Abel and Cain represent the development of human civilization in a very concrete way. Abel is a shepherd and Cain is a farmer. Cain's name may be derived from a first millennium BC word meaning "metal smith." In other words, Abel is a nomadic herdsman and Cain is a more modern man, one who has learned how to cultivate the soil and make metal tools. The story of Cain and Abel is about more than sibling rivalry in an immediate, family sense. It is also the story of conflict in the human family, the crisis that develops in human history when people begin to cultivate the soil and stop being nomads. The people who cultivate the soil can live in one place. They give up their wanderer existence and form settlements. They give up their tents for more permanent dwellings and eventually they build towns and cities.

This shift from a nomadic existence to establishing settlements made civilization possible. It was not an easy transition; it involved enormous shifts, and obviously, as the Cain and Abel story relays, conflict and violence. There were actual conflicts between farmers and nomads. We see this early human history replicated in the conflicts in the American West, between native peoples and the European invaders and settlers for whom these invaders paved the way. Later there was also conflict between ranchers and farmers as the "Old West" became more "civilized." This nomadic versus settler and rancher conflict is part of the romantic mythology of American history. From the novels by Zane Grey, to the musical *Oklahoma* and many John Wayne/John Ford films, this "range war" endures in American legends of the settlement of the West. Eventually, both in myth and history, civilization marches on, despite the perceived innocence and romance of the nomadic existence.

You could even say, then, that Cain is the founder of culture. Nomads had no need for complicated political and grandiose social systems. They operated more on familial and tribal traditions. Permanent settlements, however, require more complex social and legal systems. Conflicts over land, water rights, and a host of legal issues arise when people live permanently in an area for generations—these are the foundation of modern political systems. People build places to live, places to govern, places to trade, and places to conduct their religious rituals. Art, architecture, and religion are all part of the development of culture. The violence from which this change takes place is a critical perspective that is almost wholly absent from the romantic and positive liberal interpretations of the "march of civilization" idea of human history and cultural development, or the conservative nostalgia about a more "innocent," traditional past.

THE ABRAHAMIC CAIN

Religion manifests itself in culture, and it is also shaped by culture. It is significant that the Abrahamic religious traditions (Judaism, Christianity and Islam that revere Abraham) not only gave rise to the story of Cain and Abel, but also found this story compelling for centuries. These religious traditions formed the basis of European civilizations. European creativity manifested itself not only in the art, architecture, technology, laws, and economies its people invented, but also in aggression, particularly in colonial conquests. From Africa to the Americas (both North and South) and into Asia, this aggression overwhelmed and sometimes even destroyed other traditions that placed the natural world in a more central relationship with humans.

The story of Cain and Abel reveals the deep struggle in the cultures that sprang from this religious vision. The struggle is not between the "innocent" Abel and the "evil" Cain; the struggle is much more complex and convoluted. Human traits like aggression and selfishness, the very traits that caused Cain to kill Abel, also drove him to be creative enough to found civilization. Human creativity is both creative and destructive. Yet, we are all also Abel.

Human beings are creatures of the earth. We come from it and we'll return to it. But in the European traditions, the Cain drive is more prominent. This is the drive to conquer nature and "subdue" it.

Compare Native American religious traditions and their emphasis on the need for human harmony with the natural world. These traditions blur the distinction, so influential in the European view, between the human and the non-human.

In the Euro-Atlantic cultures, however, it is Cain who is the author of a culture that has been markedly creative as well as markedly destructive for the world. The Islamic perspective is that Cain repents. For Christianity, in particular, Cain doesn't repent; he founds Western civilization.

CREATIVITY AND DESTRUCTION

The history of Western culture illustrates the conundrum of Cain and Abel very well. This history can be told as a series of creative breakthroughs that are both enormously productive for human life and enormously destructive. The increasing creativity of these civilizations is also increasingly alienating for human beings, both from the environment and from each other.

The Agricultural Revolution

The first creative breakthrough for humanity is at the root of the biblical story of Cain and Abel. Human beings figured out that they could plant the seeds that fell from the crops they gathered and settle in one place. Some cultural anthropologists actually credit women with discovering agriculture. They speculate that since the woven baskets women used to gather plants in the hunter gatherer period of human history were slightly porous, as the women walked seeds fell from their baskets and plants grew. Somebody noticed this and agriculture was born.

But as the story of Adam and Eve illustrates, this was a crisis for humanity. One way to read the story of Adam and Eve is to read it as a community remembering a time when they didn't have to break their backs planting soil that stubbornly yields "thorns and thistles" (Genesis 4:18). They said to themselves, "Remember the good old days when we just had to walk around gathering plants and go hunting whenever we wanted? Boy, that was paradise." Like human beings throughout history, the past is remembered through rose-colored glasses. If women did invent agriculture, that's at least as good a reason as any why Eve gets the blame for getting herself and Adam kicked out of the Garden of Eden. Adam turns to her and says, "So it's *your fault* I have to work the land by the sweat of my brow instead of going hunting!"

The story of Adam and Eve and their children, Cain and Abel, is at the end of the day, a primal story about the fact that human beings are no longer nomads, innocently hunting and gathering in tribal groups. When humanity discovers agriculture, civilization is born, and that first innocence, imagined or not, is long gone.

Cities, commerce, culture, and politics are invented. At the same time, poverty, injustice, and war are also invented. Nomadic tribes may have been poor, but there were no full-blown class distinctions. Violent confrontations between tribes certainly occurred, but these skirmishes were not wars as we have come to know them. The organized violence of war and the systematic exploitation of classes of people is an invention of civilization. The biblical prophets continually rant against the kind of politics that produces poverty and injustice, especially against the most vulnerable like widows and orphans.

The scale of human exploitation went up exponentially with the next creative burst in human civilization. The outrage of the biblical prophets such as Isaiah or Jeremiah at the plight of widows and orphans in the unjust political and economic structures of their time was echoed loudly in the works of Charles Dickens and American muckrakers over the social and moral effects of the industrial revolution.

The Industrial Revolution

None of the biblical prophets could have imagined the industrial revolution. What they did know, however, is that human creativity and human pain are deeply connected. From the eighteenth to the nineteenth centuries, first in England and then spreading throughout Europe and North America, this dynamic period gave rise to modernity. Up until the 1980s, the "cause" of the industrial revolution was generally thought to have been the invention of the steam engine and from that invention the mechanization of most production, including agriculture. Now it is more the fashion to see this period not from the supply side, i.e., the burst of productivity that machines made possible, but from the side of consumption. The machine age needed markets, and markets were aggressively sought through colonial expansion.

Political and religious inventions went hand in hand with technological inventions. The Protestant Reformation supported the political discovery of the individual. In turn, political systems increased civil protections for the individual. Individual liberty led to more religious innovation, though not without struggle with civil authority. In England, for example, religious innovation spurred the study of science and mathematics. Unitarians, a dissenting religious group from the dominant Church of England, started what they called "Dissenting Academies." These academies founded and run by religious "dissenters" emphasized the study of math and science. This distinguished them from the traditional Anglican dominated schools like Oxford and Cambridge and their emphasis on Greek and Hebrew. Greek and Hebrew are not useful for the development of manufacturing technologies and thus it was the religious "dissenters" who were not economically privileged who learned the skills to help them succeed in this new modern age of math and science.

Manufacturing was not the province of the upper classes. It was "trade" and viewed as beneath the ruling class. This proved to be the basis for the eventual destruction of the feudal system as the rise of manufacturing became the root of social change. The Industrial Revolution, despite its appalling exploitation of poor and working class people, also brought about the middle class. This economic shift went hand-in-hand with profound political change. Social innovation needed a politics that rewarded innovation and thus democracy replaced aristocracy. That change as well was anything but smooth, involving domestic revolutions and war.

The mechanical age was a huge burst of creativity that changed human history. It provided more goods and services more quickly to humankind than had ever been available, but it also caused widespread suffering and death not only through poor working conditions but also through the violent expansion of these industrializing powers into new "markets." The discovery of the individual was both a political and spiritual boon to humanity.

Yet, Protestant and Catholic missions, working in conjunction with economic and political interests, helped further the subjugation and even destruction of native peoples and their indigenous traditions.

The net effect of the industrial revolution was both enormous creativity and enormous destruction. War became mechanized. World War I was the first industrialized war and the mass death in that war was a crisis for the idea that human beings were becoming more civilized through industrial progress. The Holocaust was an extreme example of the industrialization of mass death, including applying new developments in chemical technology to killing people, as well as a version of the 'assembly line' to making extermination more efficient; the Atom Bomb that obliterated Hiroshima and Nagasaki showed the world exactly what industrial progress could accomplish. Yet, ironically, atomic technology has ultimately resulted in life-saving cancer treatments. It's really not the technology; it's the people who are complicated.

As human beings became individuals in the eighteenth through the twentieth centuries, they discovered "freedom." There is a good reason why the early centuries of this period are called "The Age of Enlightenment." But freedom and individuality can also have a price. In a literal sense, some people's freedom is finally purchased with the freedom of others, if not in actual slavery, then in its economic or social equivalent. In the "Enlightenment" the dominant classes started to understand themselves more as individuals, and less as members of communities, more as "minds" and less as bodies that are part of the natural world. This period accelerated the alienation of a powerful group of people from nature, and from those who symbolize nature, women and non-dominant races.

THE DIGITAL REVOLUTION

The first computer I ever saw took up a whole room. Steve Jobs and Steve Wozniak changed that when they built the first personal computer in Jobs' parent's garage in 1976, using microprocessor technology. The invention of the personal computer and the later development of the Internet launched what we now call the digital revolution. The original research for the Internet was part of a project of the U.S. Department of Defense in 1973. But in the subsequent ten years, it became what it is today: a public, voluntary and cooperative effort of connected institutions. It is not owned by any organization or government entity.

It is almost impossible to overstate the global impact of the digital revolution. The speed with which it has evolved; its broad impact on the day-to-day lives of people around the world; its impact on the way business is conducted; and the concept of what a business is, has sent shock waves around the world. The digital revolution has, as Thomas Friedman famously observed, made the world flat. Digital communication has produced a global economy through electronic communication. This technology has made the world flat, i.e., level in terms of commerce, where Indian phone operators, for example, are employed by U.S. airlines and many other companies in customer service.[1]

A global world economy has been viewed as a good thing, spurring productivity and helping formerly disadvantaged populations become more economically competitive. In the economic meltdown that became visible in 2008, however, the flip side of globalization became all too apparent. Global financial systems are inextricably linked. The mortgage crisis and subsequent credit crises have had a huge global impact.

While the digital revolution has spurred economic productivity, it is undermining the very middle class that the industrial revolution built. This has been dubbed "Brazilification" by Douglas Coupland. "Brazilification" is a word Coupland coined to describe the widening gulf in America in recent years between the rich and the poor and the accompanying disappearance of the middle class. Brazil has already basically eradicated its middle class. Brazil has only a few mega rich and a predominately poor general population. The current economic downturn and the Wall Street bailout has greatly accelerated the "Brazilification" of the United States.

In his first novel, *Generation X: Tales for an Accelerated Culture,* Coupland gave a name and a brand to his own generation (Americans and Canadians who reached adulthood in the late 1980s), who were raised in the superheated Internet age. While Generation X stuck as a label, the irony of Coupland's social commentary was lost on the very economic and cultural drivers he skewered. The clothing company Gap, for example, tried to make him a spokesman for an ad campaign, an invitation Coupland refused. In his subsequent novels, *Shampoo Planet, Microserfs* and *jPod,* Coupland has kept his eye on the cultural and political degenerations of the electronic age. In *Microserfs,* for example, Bill Gates is a lord and the Silicon Valley serfs scurry around in a feudal-like state.[2]

The digital age has produced, a la Friedman, a great deal of economic power and productivity. Social organizing became political organizing in the Obama campaign and is widely credited with being a large part of his successful run for the presidency. The continued electronic networking of this political movement has allowed the Obama administration to go directly to the public and pressure Congress to pass legislation, though not as effectively as many had thought would be the case.

Social networking, economic productivity, and globalization are forces launched by the digital age that are at war with each other. The more connected we are to one another, the more alienated we become, both from one another and from the planet. People experience the contradiction between greater connection and greater alienation through technology every day. A 2009 movie *He's Just Not That Into You*, based on the self-help book by the same name, Mary (Drew Barrymore) discovers that the Internet is not a great place to look for romance. In fact, she laments over all the interconnected electronic devices that enable her to experience the same rejection in several different, linked electronic formats. More seriously, teenagers have to negotiate landmines of rejection in cyberspace and suicides have resulted from this stress. The phenomenon of school massacres is related to electronically enhanced rejection; the mass murderers often use the Internet to express their alienation and sense of rage.

In addition, the digital age is causing new forms of discrimination. The "digital divide" is the new class division between those who have computers and other high-tech devices, and those for whom this technology is out of reach financially. Public libraries have public access computers, but of course libraries in poor neighbourhoods are often poorly equipped. Cities and towns strapped in this financial contraction are cutting back on library services as well. The "digital divide" is a serious new class division, because those who cannot navigate the age of the Internet will be left out of the economic opportunities the digital age does generate.

It is not only on a personal level that creativity and alienation are aggravated in the digital age. The greater the economic connectivity, the greater the risk of global economic collapse. It is well to remember that it was young "geeks" who created the computer models that contributed to the recent financial meltdown by trying to "outsmart Wall Street" through complex, and ultimately financially unstable, "derivatives."[3]

If Cain is the biblical "modern man," the one who makes technology and also does violence, he has really come into his own in the digital age. The astonishing human creativity in inventing computer technology also allows humanity to wage technologically enhanced warfare where those doing the killing are at computer screens far removed from the death and destruction they are causing. This kind of warfare is nicknamed "Nintendo War" after a computer video game. Computers have also helped create one world economy; it's great when people in India can get more jobs, it's terrible when interconnected debt drives nearly the whole world into recession.

Friedman has also warned us that not only is this age "flat," it is getting *Hot, Flat and Crowded.* He says that "global warming" should be named "global weirding," as what is occurring is erratically disruptive effects produced by climate change. The global planetary crisis of climate change is a direct result of human creativity in the agricultural, industrial, and now digital ages.[4]

FREEDOM AND ANXIETY

My BlackBerry® frees me from my desktop computer, keeps me in contact with everybody all the time and effectively dominates my life. Employees complain that in the BlackBerry world, they are always working, and employers believe workers should be available 24/7. Employees report feeling torn when offered a BlackBerry or other such device as a perk at work; they are concerned that their personal lives will become nonexistent.[5] In politics, constant communication has become the norm. Even President Obama had trouble letting go of his BlackBerry, apparently. During the sabbatical in which I wrote this book, I turned off the email function on my BlackBerry and initially felt very anxious because I was imagined I was disconnected from all communication, all the time. Eventually, however, I came to realize a sense of freedom from anxiety about communication.

Oddly enough, Cain and my conflicts over my BlackBerry are connected. Cain as the new technology guy, the "metalworker," is also the one who introduces conflict and even violence into the world. In the same way, the more technology frees us, the more violence it does to human nature. The more creative and complicated the technology, the more it tempts human beings to overestimate their natures and their possibilities for transcending the one fact of human nature that nobody can finally deny. We are finite.

Freedom and anxiety are deeply related. The more we come to believe through our technologically assisted world in human transcendence, the more the anxiety of the human situation is aggravated. No matter how creative and independent of nature human beings become (or think they have become), nature ends up having the last word. Everybody dies. All religions and cultures of the world have different interpretations of this unalterable fact. In Christianity, death has been understood as a penalty for sin, as the Apostle Paul notes about the story of the Garden of Eden, death came into the world because of the disobedience of Adam and Eve. Salvation is not only salvation from sin, it is salvation from death, and promises "eternal life." This is a classical Christian view and still very much in evidence in conservative Christianity in the United States today. In the next chapter we will deal with this extensively in the concept of the "Rapture" and how it helped us get to Iraq.

One aspect of the popular culture version of the Rapture is particularly important. In the Bible, in the Book of Revelation, there is a period called the tribulation when the sinners and the saved people both suffer, *then* Christ returns for the saved people. But the popular culture "Rapture" novels have a "pre-tribulation" rapture. The saved folks get taken up before the struggles of the end time. They're out of here. These are folks who are betting they won't even die, they just believe they will be snatched up by God literally out of their socks while still alive. This is as much a denial of death as secular folks who are looking to be cryogenically frozen until science can find a cure for whatever ails them.

Modern people in Euro-Atlantic cultures, dominated as they are by technological revolutions, are more and more in denial of their own finitude. That applies to the religious and the secular, the conservative, and the liberal. The denial just takes different forms. But at the same time, we all do go to funerals. The news is full of death, local death and death in wars, famines and natural disasters near and far. So even though many people live as though death does not exist in modern technologically assisted Western culture, people still die.

The more individuals and whole societies in this religious heritage feel anxious about this seemingly irresolvable conflict, the more aggressive they become. As Reinhold Niebuhr so accurately said, "Man is insecure and involved in natural contingency; he seeks to overcome his insecurity by a will-to-power which over-reaches the limits of human creatureliness."[6] In other words, we're insecure because we know in our heart of hearts that we get sick and finally we die. That's "natural contingency." Technology has made this insecurity much worse, Niebuhr went on to argue (in 1941!) because "modern technology has tempted contemporary man to overestimate the possibility and the value of eliminating his insecurity in nature."[7] And Niebuhr didn't even have a computer, an iPod or a BlackBerry. We should realize, however, that Niebuhr writes as though these human characteristics are worldwide universal truths. That was typical of theology in his day, and frankly, of most of Western theology and philosophy up until the end of the twentieth century.

Another aspect of globalization is that Western people are in contact with others around the world and are being forced to learn that Western culture and religion are not universals. They have elements of insights and important ones at that, but in a global village other interpretations of Christianity itself have had different cultural effects. Other religions have had different cultural effects than those of the West. We all do face the same planetary threats and need the insights global perspectives can bring.

We in the United States are desperately in need of seeing ourselves as others see us, in fact, because the "will-to-power" produced by the anxiety of technologically creative modern life is a big force driving international conflict. Indeed, the rise of religious fundamentalism in the United States and around the world, is due in large part to a rising anxiety in traditional societies or segments of societies about the intrusions of modern culture into their lives and values through mass media, including the Internet.[8]

ANXIETY AND THE WILL-TO-POWER

It is well to remember that it is *insecurity*, not really security that drives the will-to-power. Cain killed Abel because he felt that his sacrifice to God was not acceptable and he became jealous and insecure. Cain built a city, but even the rise of cities and whole civilizations has not made human beings less insecure and less jealous of one another. Human nature has not changed very much, despite all the technological advances we have made. But our technological advances have made it possible for some of us to have the ability kill the rest of us. In addition, our wired world is aggravating our sense of disconnection, making us feel less secure and increasing our anxiety.

Looking at the recent past can help us uncover some layers of problems. The desire to believe we are innocent has become more and more acute in modern society because of the anxiety produced by modern life. Nothing illustrates this layering better than the religious ideas that helped us attack Iraq and decide it was okay for us as society to torture prisoners.

PART TWO

The Danger of Innocence

THREE

IRAQ AND TORTURE

Many people dream of Eden because they long to live in an innocent time when our communities and beliefs were not under attack from so many different directions. The rise of conservative religion around the world is due in large part to the disconcerting, destabilizing effects of living in a wired, globalized world.[1] Conservative religion, especially in its culturally reactionary forms, offers itself as a refuge from the anxiety of modernity—at its most extreme, it offers a return to the innocence of Eden.

The growth of conservative religion at home and abroad passed virtually unnoticed (except by the conservative religious people who saw their numbers and influence growing) in the second half of the twentieth century. Academics in particular would not give up on their idea that modernity would do away with religious belief. *Time* magazine ran its famous "Is God Dead?" cover in 1966 and intellectuals concurred—but they agreed with that idea as late as the 1990s when it was plain that Protestant evangelicalism and conservative Catholicism were becoming bigger and bigger factors in American public life. Right up until 9/11, books and articles were still predicting the "triumph" of secularism over religion.

That is how a massive build-up of religious conservatism both in the United States and in the Islamic world crept up on so many of us. There were warning signs, but very few intellectuals heeded them.

Here's what's really happening: religion, especially conservative religion, is not only not going away, it is growing. Conservative religion is growing in power and influence not only in the United States but also around the world. The election of Barack Obama, perhaps one of the most devout Christians elected to the Presidency in many years, did not end that trend. It just added the race factor and that confuses a lot of people, especially white liberals, who have very little experience or understanding of the black religious experience in America.

Understanding just how dangerous a radically conservative answer to modernity can be, especially in its message of a promised return to innocence, is absolutely critical to formulate a *religious answer* to the problems of modern life. I hate to break it to the academics and state department folks and others who are still hoping secularism is on the rise—secularism is dead. Around the world, people are turning to religious explanations for human existence and human meaning, and are turning away from reason, science, and materialism as the sole source of their meaning and truth. The only choice we have now is what kind of religious case we can make to people to deal with the real problems of modernity. And it must *be* a religious argument, a way of talking about meaning and purpose that actually helps people. That means it must be an answer that draws on our deepest religious narratives, like the Garden of Eden and the fall from innocence. The previous chapter gave a short history of what happened to biblical Cain in western culture. If that experience is a reliable guide, the problems caused by modernity are only going to get worse. Anxiety is on the rise and it is very toxic.

HIGH ANXIETY

On March 19, 2003, the United States attacked Iraq, a country that had not attacked us. Approximately two weeks earlier, as the national debate over whether or not to attack Iraq had reached a fever pitch,[2] I found myself one of six people invited to debate the idea of attacking Iraq in a nationally televised *Nightline* Special Town Meeting in Washington, DC.

The site chosen was an Episcopal church across the street from the White House. On the panel with me were Joe Wilson, the former U.S. Ambassador to Iraq (married to Valerie Plame), Rev. Richard Land, a Baptist minister and the President of the Ethics and Religious Liberty initiative of the Southern Baptist Convention, James Woolsey, former Director of the CIA, John McCain, Republican Senator from Arizona, and Carl Levin, Democratic Senator from Michigan. The title of the program was "Why Now?"

Those on the panel who were in favor of attacking Iraq were McCain, Woolsey, and Land. They stated that Saddam had "weapons of mass destruction" and he would use them to attack us at any moment. But, of course, now we know that there were no weapons of mass destruction in Iraq. It is now clear from more recent research and documents that the Bush Administration actually knew, or strongly suspected this was the case, and knew before we attacked Iraq.[3]

Americans really are often tempted to see themselves as innocent, even (or perhaps especially) when they are about to go to war. The nuclear threat (as well as the biological weapons threat—the so called package of 'Weapons of Mass Destruction') was critical to justifying attacking Iraq, a country that had not attacked us, and still claim we were innocent. During the *Nightline* town meeting, one shrill young woman in the audience asked me a very emotional question about 'which U.S. city was I willing to sacrifice?' to a nuclear bomb unless we attacked Iraq.

The case for attacking Iraq because of a pending nuclear threat was helped enormously by the rise of religious conservatism and its seeding the culture for decades with apocalyptic interpretations of global strife. This certainly started with the Cold War and "godless Communism" rhetoric, but continued with greater and greater emphasis on nuclear conflict as the way God would bring about the end of history. Then, when America watched the huge plumes of smoke rise from the devastation of the World Trade Center's twin towers in New York, the case practically made itself. Every childhood fear of the mushroom cloud generated by our schoolroom 'duck and cover' practice, every nuclear disaster movie, indeed the "Sum of All Fears," was marshalled to get Americans to accept the morality of attacking Iraq.

The American people had become convinced over years of work by religious conservatives who understood far better and far earlier than liberals how much people long to escape the threat of modern life and return to an innocent world. For a quarter of a century, Christian conservatives were spreading the message that a Christian America was the answer to the threats posed in an increasingly complex and dangerous world. They did a very good job of convincing religious Americans that they were innocent and that preserving their security at any price was the ultimate righteousness. They were especially good at linking that interpretation to the nuclear threat. When 9/11 happened, the case was already made.

HOW WE GOT TO IRAQ

We did not get to Iraq overnight. Big cultural shifts had to take place in order for us to be willing to attack a country that had not attacked us first. And religion was a big factor in the cultural shifts. It was conservative, not liberal or even mainstream religion that influenced the cultural sea change. After the end of the Vietnam War, many mainstream Christians produced theologies of peace. The American Catholic Bishops issued their well-stated rejection of nuclear weapons use, *The Challenge of Peace: God's Promise and Our Response.* Many Protestant denominations issued statements on peace including the United Church of Christ's *A Just Peace Church* (1986), as well as statements by the United Methodists and the Presbyterian Church USA.

I was an author and the editor of the United Church of Christ statement on *A Just Peace Church.* I have now come to believe that those of us who worked so hard on outlining a case for ending war because it had become too destructive for humanity and the environment were also tempted by innocence. We did not see what else was happening in religion and culture, or when we did, we didn't take it seriously enough. We fell into the liberal trap of thinking that if only people would see the good of peace, they would make peace. We failed to learn the lesson of Cain: society is very unstable and difficult for people and they want to impose some meaning on it so they won't always be scared to death.

While religious liberals were writing peace theologies, religious conservatives such as Hal Lindsey or John Wesley White, an associate of the Billy Graham crusade, were busily seeding the idea of a God of wrath who will use nuclear weapons to punish sinful humanity and save the innocent believers. Lindsey's *The Late Great Planet Earth,* a fictional account of a nuclear war that

Won

brings in the Second Coming of Christ, sold more copies than any other book in the 1970s, including the Bible.

One of the most important cultural as well as religious aspects of Lindsay's work was the writing on the "Rapture." The Rapture refers to the joy a true believer will experience when Christ returns for them and instantly "catches up" all the believers and translates them into their immoral bodies.[4]

Lindsey and the other conservative Christians who write on the Rapture start from the idea that people in general are really, really bad due to the disobedience of Adam [and Eve]. This is very much in line with the traditional Christian conservative view of the Garden of Eden and the "fall." These conservatives contend that sinful, disobedient humans deserve punishment and a wrathful God is going to punish them in a very violent way.

my student

But what's new for the popular Christian conservatives who write about the Rapture is this innovation: the great thing for the true believer is that he or she will get to *skip* all that punishment and go directly to heaven. The true believer gets restored to innocence in the Rapture. And, conveniently enough, gets to understand him or herself as innocent (i.e., saved) in this life as well. As is described below, this is a genuinely innovative idea on the part of the far Right; it is not classical Christian doctrine and it is certainly not what the Book of Revelation in the New Testament actually says about the end times.

One central idea in this conservative idea of the Rapture is that there really are two kinds of human nature. Some human beings, according to these religious conservatives, are dreadful sinners who deserve to be punished. Other human beings, the "saved," are good and will be snatched up before the punishment starts. But all this takes place at the end of history, so in the meantime there are sheep and goats, the saved and the unsaved, the innocent and the guilty, living side by side here and now. This obviously creates a lot of tension and even conflict in human society. The innocent and the guilty don't normally see things eye-to-eye, especially when it comes to politics.

Through popular books, the Rapture has become a part of how people make meaning in this violent and chaotic world. It is surprising (to some) that more than half (55 percent) of Americans reply to pollsters that they believe in the Rapture. With the advent of the Internet, Rapture theology really took off. (You can track the progress of the rapture at www.raptureready.com in case you'd like to know how close to the end times we are.)

The work toward consolidating the conservative religious interpretation of American culture and religion was there to see in the religious rhetoric of the Cold War, especially with President Reagan's "Evil Empire" description of the Soviet Union. Obviously, the Communists are secularists, therefore among the "unsaved" and deserving of God's wrath. But Reagan's view of the Russians as big sinners by and large had no effect on policy. In the Reagan presidency, the foreign policy establishment moved on its professional way during that era, employing deterrence and the real politik of containment without much impact from President Reagan's theological views.

And then the Soviet Union fell and for a brief moment, the United States contemplated a "peace dividend." But that was only on the surface. For a short time, the country rode the Internet highway to huge economic productivity; that's why academics in the 1990s were still deluding themselves that religion, especially conservative religion, would just go away. Human history looked like it was progressing nicely. Liberal innocence and optimism was on the rise in the 1990s, at least until the Bill Clinton sex scandal erupted and the dot-com bubble burst.

Conservatives worked hard to develop and spread their cultural and religious story during the Bill Clinton era. They were really motivated by Clinton; social progress in gay rights, a woman's right to choose, and at least the idea of universal health care were regarded as very wrong. When reproductive choice was combined with the sexual behavior of the president, this absolutely demonstrated to the religious right that these progressive ideas were sinful. The political work of the Clinton presidency, especially the increase in taxes on wealthier Americans, so enraged the political right that it drove coalition-building between the religious right and the political right even faster than before.

In 1995, Tim LaHaye and Jerry B. Jenkins published *Left Behind: A Novel of the Earth's Last Days*. It is the first in what has become a series of wildly popular books on the Rapture. More than 60,000,000 copies of the books in this series have been sold worldwide. The enormous popularity of these books (and the Rapture films, videogames, and comics) are why more than half of Americans think history will end in the violent return of Christ for the innocent, true believers, and the sinful will go straight to hell.

The premise of the *Left Behind* books is that the Rapture has already occurred and the believers have gone to heaven. Remember the authors of these popular books are pushing the new, improved version of the end of history idea. In their new, improved (and not biblical version) the innocent believers get a free pass version of the Rapture. They get to leave town and then all the sinners have to deal with the mess because they are "left behind" with problems of "global weirding," or immigration, or health care, or the need to take care of our national infrastructure before more bridges fall down. But only the guilty, those "left behind," have to worry about that.

This new, non-biblical version of the Rapture, one that does not conform to what the biblical Book of Revelations says about what will happen as the end times approach, makes perfect sense if what you want to do is convince the true believers that they are so good that God is not going to allow them to struggle or suffer even during the return of Christ. This is a very optimistic view of human nature for some people (the saved) surrounded by an incredibly pessimistic and violent interpretation of the rest of humanity as well as the nature of God. It is also an interpretation that fuels an "us versus them" view of society and, as Rick Perlstein has written, a "politics of anger."[5]

The overlap between the Clinton era and the plot of the *Left Behind* series is enormously instructive. As the first book in the *Left Behind* series begins, a pilot is flying an airplane, while at the same time lusting in his heart for the first flight attendant. The pilot is startled out of his revere by the news that people on the plane are disappearing, leaving neat piles of their clothing behind. After some difficulty, the pilot, who has not disappeared, manages to land the plane amid great chaos. All around the world people become aware that millions have simply disappeared. Some speculate that this was an alien attack, but the small group of main characters in the novel are convinced that those who disappeared experienced the "Rapture" as the Book of Revelation in the Bible describes it and the disappeared have really gone to heaven.

Other signs that the era of biblical prophecy is at hand become apparent. Just weeks before Israel had been attacked by Russian, Iraqi, and Syrian forces. The attack fails, however, because when planes come to drop bombs on Jerusalem, they simply fall harmlessly from the sky. This is taken as evidence that biblical prophecy is being fulfilled because God is protecting Jerusalem.

The pilot (who is married) and is "lusting" after the flight attendant may be a reference to Bill Clinton, who while governor and then president, faced accusations of extra-marital affairs. But it is also the case that Christian conservatives also found Bill Clinton a source of "tribulation" because of Clinton's support, again as governor though, of course, later as president, of women's reproductive rights. During the Clinton presidency, his administration's work in peace-making diplomacy in the Middle East was also a source of tribulation to religious conservatives. Clinton's peace initiative was not viewed with joy by the fundamentalists (nor, of course, by political conservatives who considered this yet another example of Clinton being "weak" on foreign policy). Armed conflict in the Middle East is central to the fundamentalist theological premise that war in the Middle East will hasten the fulfilment of biblical prophecy. Peace in the Middle East will only delay this process. During the actual (i.e., not fictional) conflict between Israel and Hezbollah, the index of Rapture on www.raptureready.com shot up dramatically.

The main characters of the original *Left Behind* (1995) novel realize they have made a huge mistake in not being true believers and they find God and join a community of "tribulation saints." But the work of Satan in the tribulation is well underway, led by Satan-in-disguise, the head of the United Nations. Through the United Nations, Nicolae Carpathia, aka Satan, is bent on world domination. Conservative political opposition to the work of the United Nations per se, and the work of the Clinton administration's Secretary of State, Madeleine Albright (former U.S. representative to the U.N.)[6] in pursuing diplomacy especially in the Middle East is clearly evidenced in this series of novels. John Bolton, the second-term George W. Bush appointee to the U.N., seemed to have as his chief credential for the job of U.S.

representative to the U.N. contempt for the United Nations and its work.

The original *Left Behind* book was first published during the "tribulation" period when the Christian right had to endure Bill Clinton and political progressivism. The novels are about a time before the final Apocalypse and the end of history in a violent war. And then came 9/11. The religious imagination of the right made full use of this new era where America's enemies, no longer the "godless communists," in fact worshipped another God and could be safely regarded as absolutely fallen and the consummate sinners.

9/11: WHEN EVERYTHING CHANGED

The aerial photos of the smoke and debris filled plumes that rose from the collapsed towers of the World Trade Center needed no further interpretation to evoke images of the apocalypse and the end times. Rev. Jerry Falwell, fundamentalist and television evangelist, famously said on his program, *The 700 Club*, in response to the 9/11 attacks, "I really believe that the pagans, and the abortionists, and the feminists, and the gays and the lesbians who are actively trying to make that an alternative lifestyle, the ACLU, People for the American Way, all of them who have tried to secularize America. I point the finger in their face and say 'you helped this happen.'"[7] This is a logical and clear presentation of the theology of the conservative right. People who are sinners deserve the wrath of God, and a wrathful God will give it to them, big time.

After heavy criticism *from the Right*, as well as from the left, Falwell apologized. But why would the conservative Christians criticize Falwell for saying that 9/11 was God's punishment on sinful America? Falwell had made the mistake of offering the older, fundamentalist view that God's wrath will fall on the just and the unjust alike at the end of days. Falwell was criticized by religious conservatives for not offering the new, "innocent" version of the end times that was so appealing to the increasing evangelical rank-and-file. What Christian evangelical wants that old "Hell Fire and Brimstone" suffering when you can get out of it while the getting is good? Falwell showed that he was no longer in the mainstream of Christian conservatism when he issued this famous diatribe. After Falwell's death this was one of the most frequently quoted statements in comments on the meaning of his passing. His passing was rightly regarded as the end of a religious era.

The most common interpretation by religious conservatives was not Falwell's view that God was punishing the United States through the attacks of 9/11. Instead, the attacks were interpreted as the work of evildoers who "hate us because we are free."[8] Or, more plainly, 'how dare they take advantage of our innocence this way?' The conservative political idea of American innocence matches the conservative religious idea almost exactly. The political version is that our motives in foreign policy are always pure and unselfish, directed toward spreading freedom and democracy around the world, and therefore only those who hate freedom and are therefore anti-democratic would object, or even oppose us. The religious interpretation ups the ante because it introduces the idea of evil for evil's sake into the conflict. This religious view is the one that is portrayed in the opening scene of *The Passion of the Christ* when the devil makes an appearance and looms threateningly over the praying Jesus, while a snake crawls toward him, clearly intent on harm. Only Satan and his minions would hate innocence and want to destroy it precisely because it is innocent and pure.

Bush

The President's State of the Union address that followed most closely upon the events of 9/11 was written by Michael Gerson who had majored in theology at the very conservative Wheaton College. It was clear to this presidential speechwriter that the self-described evangelical president wanted a fundamental reorientation in American foreign and defense policy. The vehicle would be good versus evil, the saved (now including the entire United States) and the damned (the terrorists). The theme of guilt versus innocence went global. The innocent United States was attacked by the bad Islamists who "hate us for our freedom."[9]

PREEMPTIVE WAR

All of this conservative religious writing and speech making can be seen in American culture and politics in recent decades, but did it actually have any role in the administration deciding to attack Iraq? In other words, did religious innocence actually become dangerous? Some think it did and some think that is over-estimating the role of conservative religion in what was a pretty standard political (mis) calculation. Bob Woodward's interview with President Bush on what he was thinking at the moment of this decision seems to indicate yes, especially Bush's acknowledgment that he was praying that he would have the "strength to do the Lord's will."[10] For other commentators, conservative religious views played virtually no role, at least none worth mentioning, in the decision to attack Iraq and in the conduct of the war. *The Washington Post*'s senior Pentagon correspondent, Thomas E. Ricks, extensively researched and documented the decision to go to war as well as how it has been run in his book *Fiasco: The American Military Adventure in Iraq.*[11] Ricks does not address the role of religion in any way in this volume; he comes closest with describing the ideological rigidity of Paul Wolfowitz and Wolfowitz's conviction, out of his family's losses in the Holocaust, that there is no compromise with "evil."[12]

The way in which Americans came to believe that attacking Iraq was the right thing to do had little to do with military calculations, per Ricks' analysis, and far more to do with Wolfowitz's view that you can't negotiate with "evil." The only thing you can do with evil, in the conservative religious view, is try to kill it. The case for attacking Iraq was made during the years before the concerted effort to convince the American public that attacking Iraq was the right thing to do. The previous decades were when religious conservatives continuously pounded on the theme that there are some people who are so sinful and evil they deserve punishment (now translated as Saddam and his minions). The case for attacking Iraq was also made because these same conservatives had drummed into the American people that there are some nations so innocent and good that God is on their side (in this case, the United States led by a true-believing president). This is how we as Americans finally went along with what has now been shown to be a colossal mistake, the decision to attack Iraq.

WHEN INNOCENCE BECOMES DANGEROUS: THE DECISION TO TORTURE

The idea that the United States is innocent in its motives has been unbearably strained by the fact that torture became policy. Ironically enough, however, it is this very conviction of innocence that led us to delude ourselves that torture, if we used it, would be okay because American security is the ultimate righteousness.

On May 4, 2004, pictures started to circulate on the Internet of Iraqis detained at Abu Ghraib prison in positions that were clearly torture. One man was shown standing on a box, with a black hood over his head and wires attached to his limbs. It was later revealed he had been threatened with electrocution if he stepped off the box. Nearly naked prisoners were piled in humiliating positions, some showed signs of physical abuse, and many were in painful stress positions. Americans in military uniform were shown in these pictures as well, some smiling, one giving a thumbs-up gesture.[13] While these horrific photos were racing around the world on the Internet, I published an editorial in the *Chicago Tribune* entitled *Can a Nation Lose Its Soul? Coming to Terms with the Conscience of the United States and the Torture of Iraqi Prisoners.* The editorial was printed in the paper alongside one of the photos, the hooded prisoner attached to wires.

For more than a year, Amnesty International had been documenting the torture of Iraqis by coalition forces. Charges of abuse kept resurfacing throughout 2003 and into early 2004. And then, in January of 2004, Specialist Joseph Darby delivered a series of photos to investigators in the Criminal Division. Darby said he had been so disturbed by the photos of the abuse at Abu Ghraib prison, photos that had been given to him by one of the soldiers who appeared in the photos, that he felt it violated "everything I believed in."

What has subsequently been determined is that the administration, in the persons of its president, vice-president, and legal counsel, had decided that this country did not have to abide by the terms of the Geneva Conventions. Through a series of confidential legal memos, a spurious line of legal argument that the United States did not have to follow the Convention in the case of "enemy combatants" was developed. Jane Mayer, who, as a journalist and writer for *The New Yorker*, doggedly pursued these memos and through extensive interviews with principals documented that the torture was, from the beginning, not the work of a 'few bad apples,' but administration policy at the highest levels.

To have a rigorous concept of "human rights" you have to see other people as human. The conservative theological view of "big sinners" and "the innocent people" actually helped in the justification of torture. An "enemy combatant," in this view, is not really a person, let alone innocent until proved guilty. An enemy combatant is by definition not innocent. Thus an "enemy combatant" deserves America's and God's worst wrath. What is even more dangerous than the idea that the enemy is evil, however, is the idea that America's innocence is absolute and cannot not damaged by any acts done to keep it safe.

Every major world religion and civilized nation condemns torture and forbids it. There were those individuals who struggled against this wholesale gutting of the bedrock of American principles such as Joe Margulies, a lawyer who eventually succeeded in representing Mamdouh Habib. Habib was one of the many who were sent to Egypt and to other countries in the region, what is called "being rendered," and tortured without any hard evidence of guilt. Marguilies said, "I got the sense that America had lost its moral bearings."

But the clearest public theological condemnation of torture comes from those who have interrogated and who have seen what torture does, and not just to the tortured. Daniel Coleman, an ex-FBI agent who worked closely with the CIA, argued in vain for traditional methods of interrogation including gaining the subject's trust and affording them due process. The latter was especially effective, argued Coleman. "The lawyer's show these guys there's a way out…It's human nature. People don't cooperate with you unless they have some reason to." But after 9/11 Coleman saw that everything, including legality, had changed and that whatever they did, including extraordinary brutality, was not only legal, it was acceptable. Coleman knew differently. "Brutalization doesn't work. We know that. Besides, you lose your soul."[14]

Coleman was not the only one to realize that in adopting torture, what the United States was doing, in the person of those assigned to torture, was soul murder, not only of the tortured, but the torturer. One officer, quoted by Mayer, noted the impact on his friend of having to water board Khalid Sheikh Mohammed. His friend has nightmares, he revealed. "When you cross over that line of darkness, it's hard to come back. You lose your soul."[15]

Since the evidence of torture became public, many have tried to cover up the fundamental moral and legal problem by engaging in debates about the definition of torture. The contemporary debate is about the difference between "coercion" or "extreme interrogation" and torture. These two euphemisms have appeared frequently since the pictures from Abu Ghraib appeared.

We have lost so much in this war. We have not lost as much as the Iraqis, or those whom we mistreated as non-persons, the so-called "enemy combatants." But in addition to what we have lost financially and even morally, in going to a view of human nature that divides people into the "innocent" and the "guilty," we have lost a sense of us.

BEYOND "24"

Frequent churchgoers report the highest level of acceptance that torture is okay, the Pew research group[16] reported in the spring of 2009.[17] This research is actual evidence that religious views that convince Americans they are "innocent" do highly influence attitudes toward whether torture is okay.

But it is not only conservative religion that has led half of the American people to report that they think torture is okay "some" or "most" of the time.[18] Popular culture, especially the television show *24* on the Fox Network has been enormously influential in helping to convince the American people that torture is okay. In fact, *24* has probably been more influential in convincing Americans not only that they are justified in torturing suspects, but that it's just whining liberals that object to torture. This hit show starred Kiefer Sutherland as "Jack Bauer," the head of a counter-terrorism unit. It generally featured at least *one torture scene per episode.* The torture included shooting "terrorists" in the kneecap, chopping off their hands, or even biting them to death.

In the fourth season, Bauer was forced to 'go rogue' and leave the counter-terrorism unit because somebody from "Amnesty Global" [a barely disguised "Amnesty International"] showed up and had the nerve to make a fuss about the Geneva Conventions. In order to break the suspect's fingers, Jack had to become a private citizen. Of course, breaking someone's fingers is also illegal when you're a private citizen, but that kind of logic does not make it into these bizarre scripts.

The explicit connection between this fictional show and real conservative political strategy became especially clear in 2006 when Homeland Security Chief Michael Chertoff appeared alongside the show's producers and three cast members at an event sponsored by the Heritage Foundation to discuss 'The public image of US terrorism policy.' The discussion was moderated by Rush Limbaugh. You can get a video of this inspiring event at the C-SPAN store.[19]

24 was launched in November 2001, two months after the attacks of 9/11. It ran for years, except for a hiatus during the writer's strike. The show has made the torture case for years that former Vice President Dick Cheney was trying to make on his rounds of the talk shows in the spring of 2009. The idea that kept being made by the fictional Jack Bauer of *24* and the real, former Vice President was that torture is necessary to "keep America safe" and it "works." It's always some "ticking bomb" problem that can only be solved by information obtained under torture. In order words, 'you terrorists made us do it.' Otherwise, American innocence would have prevented us from doing these things. The moral argument is that this war crime is justified because it 'keeps America safe.' Both the character Jack Bauer and the real person, Dick Cheney, present themselves as the "good guys." This is about as dangerous as the illusion of innocence gets. It can even get you to commit war crimes.

There are some, including President Barack Obama, who want to go "forward" and not deal with the mess "left behind" by torture, rendition, and violations of American civil rights, as well as the rights of prisoners under the Geneva Conventions. Indeed, in the winter of Obama's second year in office, his Justice Department's report on the role of the lawyers who authored the torture memos concluded the memos showed "poor judgment" but did not constitute a crime.[20] Thus we have been so far left with no actual confrontation, on the part of the nation, with the fundamental error of torture as a crime against humanity, and we are still without a concerted legal way to address this crime and its consequences.

Dealing with torture and the false pretexts for the attack on Iraq, however, are about correcting the fundamental error of American innocence. The idea of American innocence is still widespread in American culture. The staggering statistics on how many Americans still approve of torture more than documents that. Establishing a real alternative means avoiding both the errors of liberal innocence as well as the errors of conservative innocence. It is crucial that we understand the dangers of innocence in order to construct a genuine religious *and political* alternative.

Yes, we are not in the Garden of Eden any more. But that is not bad news, religiously speaking. We need to know that we are not innocent, but we also need to know that we're not just damned sinners either. But before we reconstruct the Garden of Eden story of the "fall" from innocence in a way that can actually help us, however, we should look at another concrete example of when innocence becomes dangerous. This example is about the illusion that financial markets are innocent. This idea works especially well in a market economy like we have here in the United States. Translated into economic language, for the "good people" greed is good and regulation is bad. And the "bad people" are really just getting what they deserve in terms of lost jobs or homes. When Jenkins or LaHay write books called *Left Behind* one of the things they really mean is that in *this world* the poor people (and the unsaved middle class) *get left behind.* That's the dollars and cents version of the Rapture. The conservative religious idea that there are innocent people and guilty people is alive and well in the efforts to blame the economic meltdown on the poor and middle class.

Market economies are far from innocent; at best they drive innovation and create jobs. But remember Cain—Cain, the murderer, invented civilization. I'm sure one of the first things Cain did after founding the first city was start trading and creating markets. That's part of the human story of creation, and destruction. Markets cannot be innocent—they are driven by human desire, especially the desire for acquisition.

FOUR

FINANCIAL MELTDOWN

Greed, for lack of a better word, is good.

—Gordon Gekko in *Wall Street.*

Oliver Stone's[1] 1987 film, *Wall Street,* proved to be positively prophetic as the U.S. economy went into a meltdown in the fall of 2008. Stone made this film during the Reagan era (1980–1992). In the film, the character Gordon Gekko was the greedy Wall Street speculator, and justified his creed of greed with both charm and a hint of malice. It's clear that no good can come from this. In real life, however, the creed of greed has dominated for decades on Wall Street and been given ethical cover by the idea that the market is guided by an "invisible hand" and thus its profit-making is always good.

Stephen Colbert of *Comedy Central* has skewered this view with precision. He calls the belief in the goodness of markets "moneytheism."[2] A play on "monotheism" (belief in one God), "moneytheism," as explained by Colbert, is a deeply held belief that free-market capitalism is guided by an invisible force that will mysteriously ensure that everything works out for the best (i.e., people at the top make money).

Beyond the failure of regulators, or Wall Street greed, or mortgage companies who offered mortgages to people who couldn't afford them, one of the things we need to challenge is the idea that a market economy itself is innocent. It is hard to challenge this idea because a booming market economy is essential to our American lifestyle. We want our market economy to work. And so, we are tempted.

The current market meltdown has generated surprisingly little anger at Wall Street; instead, populist anger, especially by "Tea Party" activists, is directed at "government regulation." This demonstrates just how strong is the American belief in the almost divine nature of markets and their capacity, if left unregulated, to deliver continual boom-times. The source of this temptation is twofold: first, we want it so much, and second, conservative Christianity constantly reinforces the idea that the market is good and innocent. Unfortunately, it is this very faith in the innocence of markets that will keep us from enforcing realistic regulations to keep the booms from going bust, as they have for decades.

Economic booms are the result of people falling into temptation, believing what they want to believe, seeing only what they want to see and deceiving themselves and others. Economists don't call this "temptation"; they call it "bubbles." Economist Robert Shiller argues that the huge speculative booms should be called "bubbles" because no information from outside the bubble can get in when the bubble is expanding. To me, this is like a child without an immune system who must live in a bubble. No germs from outside the bubble can get in to harm the child in the bubble.

The problem is, the kind of out-of-control speculative bubbles that dominate the U.S. economy with more and more frequency, also are sealed up and no information from outside the bubble can get in. Shiller says these kinds of bubbles are fueled by "contagious optimism, seemingly impervious to facts, that often takes hold when prices are rising. Bubbles primarily are a social phenomena; until we understand and address the psychology that fuels them, they're going to keep forming."[3]

These "social phenomena" are also "religious phenomena" in the sense that people have faith in the U.S. markets. People want to think that the capitalist system is good and only good can come from booming markets. People want to believe not only in their own innocence, but also in the innocence of the economic system that drives our way of life. This is not really an economic system; it's a belief system.[4] Belief in the innocence of the markets persists despite all evidence because the faith in the markets *is inside the bubble.* Alan Greenspan, who was Chairman of the Federal Reserve for almost twenty years, had huge faith in the markets. After the meltdown, people in the business community wondered how someone as knowledgeable as Greenspan could think that the " 'bubble' would never burst."[5]

It is not simply the innocence of markets that drove Greenspan's views. Inside the bubble is the faith in human innocence, the idea that people actually act rationally and make rational economic decisions based on evidence. In testimony before Congress about the crisis, Greenspan said that he thought, "Market participants would be wise enough to maximize their own interest and would therefore self-regulate."[6]

Self-regulation, of all the ideas that led the U.S. economy downhill, is perhaps the biggest bubble of all. If we learned anything from "Story A," that is, the story of the desire for more that is at the heart of the Garden of Eden lesson, then we know that the "self" can't be trusted all the time to regulate itself. The "self" will be tempted by greed and arrogance and even by wishful thinking (the bubble!) to grasp at more than is good for the individual, and certainly for more than is good for the economic system as a whole. Self-regulation is the fallacy at the heart of the belief in the goodness and innocence of unfettered free markets, and the fallacy at the heart of the belief in the goodness and innocence of the people who make economic decisions that drive those markets. People on Wall Street are just like people on Main Street—they're human beings.

The idea that "economic man" will act rationally and choose to act in his own best interest is a belief system; at its heart it is completely irrational, the point that Shiller makes with great precision. When you really want to believe in something, you develop a certainty that is impervious to facts. During an interview on *60 Minutes,* while Greenspan was promoting his memoir, *The Age of Turbulence,* he said he was aware of the subprime lending practices and how adjustable rates could become a shock to the economic system, but he didn't think it would cause that much harm overall. "While I was aware a lot of these practices [subprime lending] were going on, I had no notion of how significant they had become until very late...I didn't get it until very late in 2005 and 2006."[7] What can we learn from the fact that the man who was the chief architect of American fiscal policy admitted he didn't get it? Greenspan was inside the bubble and he didn't believe that practices of subprime lending could be disastrous for the American economy if left unchecked. There is no "rational economic man." There are only men and women and they are capable of creativity and destruction, just like Adam and Eve, or Cain and Abel.

EXCESS

"Then Jesus entered the temple and drove out all who were selling and buying in the temple, and he overturned the tables of the money changers..." (Matthew 21:12). When Jesus drove the moneychangers out of the Temple in Jerusalem, he took on the brokers (bankers) who were ripping off the pilgrims who came to Jerusalem during Passover. These brokers were in cahoots with the priestly class who ran the Temple and together they would cheat pilgrims out of the fair price for their offerings. The bankers would sell their own Temple coinage in exchange for foreign money at a very high rate of exchange.

The Temple in Jerusalem was in a sense the national bank of Israel in Jesus' time; it was a powerful national treasury that did not let its great wealth sit idle. The bank loaned the money it collected *at very high interest rates.* These unjust lending practices drove many residents into extreme poverty and created the vast slums of Jerusalem. The Jewish historian Josephus, writing less than a generation after the time of Jesus, told of the huge debts owed by the poor to the rich in Jerusalem.

Jesus plainly thought that greed was evil. Jesus went so far as to physically disrupt the largest national bank in Israel by "driving out all who sold and bought in the Temple" and by overturning "the tables of the money-changers" (Matthew 21:12) during the height of Passover. Jesus directly challenged the Temple practices of ripping off poor and even more affluent pilgrims. Temple practices that charged the poor high interest rates and drove them into debt were the target of Jesus' anger. Josephus also reported that in his time, the poor rose up and burned down the building in Jerusalem where all the records of debt were kept.

The practice of exploiting the poor and the middle class is not new; what is new today, however, is that in the mid-twentieth century in the United States we figured that out and introduced realistic regulations to oversee lending practices and reign in the sinful human impulse of greed and exploitation. The Great Depression of the 1930s was in part a result of Herbert Hoover's over-confidence that business would regulate itself. After the

Depression, regulations were put in place to restrain the most extreme and risky practices of financial markets. The Great Depression was a time when the danger of innocence was low because the risks of living were so high.

These regulations from the Depression era were in place until the "Reagan Revolution" and the tide of free market economics that nearly drowned the American economy. James K. Galbraith, the Lloyd M. Bentsen, Jr., Professor of Government/ Business Relations at the University of Texas in Austin, placed the blame for the recent market meltdown squarely on deregulation. "Revolutions devour their children. Deregulation has been the public faith of the financial sector since Reagan. Under Bush II, waves of predatory finance in housing were aggressively promoted by Alan Greenspan, by McCain's closest economic adviser Phil Gramm, and by so-called regulators who systematically subvert the public interest." Paul Krugman said that as chairman of the Banking Committee, Phil Gramm bore at lot of responsibility for the credit crisis and he should be kept far away from any recovery strategies. "We could have another Great Depression if we really work at it and Phil Gramm is the guy to do it."

But the current multi-sector meltdown that began in 2008 is not merely the result of deregulation, but a failure to create new regulation for new financial instruments that, for example, allowed lenders to transfer their credit risks, i.e., mortgage defaults, to third parties and passing the losses on, creating what has been called "a massive global gamble." Add this chain reaction to the fact that high-risk mortgage loans, even "piggyback" loans where a loan for a down payment is "piggybacked" on top of the first mortgage were allowed, and the risk becomes even greater. The gamble was that the credit house of cards built on greed would not fall. It fell.

Markets themselves are not ethical instruments; they are not "self-regulating." They are *not* innocent. Markets are driven by the desire for acquisition. Regulations are designed to limit destruction wrought by greed, while not stifling the productivity of markets. It is only realistic to assume that people will take advantage and try to manipulate the system to their own financial advantage, even when this manipulation is so risky it could bring down the economy. Even good people will take these kinds of risks, convincing themselves that they are only making the financial system more productive. People don't only lie to each other and to regulators, they lie to themselves.

The failure here is to forget the huge role that temptation plays in human affairs. We really do live after the "fall" from innocence. People are tempted by the prospect of increasing profits and they are tempted to disregard the public interest for their own interest (or delude themselves that the two are interchangeable). Remember it was during the liberal presidency of Bill Clinton that the rest of the market deregulation was accomplished. Neither the extreme conservative views of human nature nor the optimistic faith in human nature of liberalism takes into account the enduring capacity of human beings to mess up and mess up badly. Both extreme conservatives and extreme liberals are tempted by the romantic notion of innocence. The conservatives don't account for the fact that *everyone* can be tempted to excess, and liberals tend to discount the role of temptation in human life and history.

That is why a new Garden of Eden story is so important for getting us to stagger along in the middle, and not fall into the dangers of innocence on the left or the right. We dare not think about human nature in a vacuum. We need to think about people concretely and in real situations. And it's not just individuals, a "few bad apples" who do bad things, that we have to watch out for. It is far more revealing to think about human sin in context, especially a sin like greed. Certain conditions conspire to tempt people to be greedy and those conditions are part of how we think about innocence and guilt. When you confine discussions about innocence and guilt to universals or generalities, you can miss the main point. What kinds of conditions led to *this* housing market crash, to *this* oil price spike and where, individually and collectively, do the responsibilities lie?

The fact human beings *do fall into temptation* is an idea that can be helpful in thinking about the American economy and how we can prevent the *next economic meltdown.* Low interest rates were one big factor in the temptation for greed among mortgage lenders. Greenspan, when he was Federal Reserve Chairman, was not being evil in continuing to lower interest rates; he wanted to keep the economy growing even though the country was pursuing a war and paying for that war on credit. Perhaps his political bosses told him, "Keep the economy humming." Who knows? All we know is that, for example, in 2001, we saw news stories that stated "In an effort to battle U.S. market conditions this year, Greenspan has been forced to roll up his sleeves and unleash five percentage cuts in the Federal funds rate. This drop from 6.5 percent to 4 percent is unheard of and the current rate is at its lowest level in seven years!"

"Hurray!" said the banks. Let's make money off these low interest rates and package lots of attractive mortgages. But the banks added to the conditions that tempted people to be greedy, because they didn't just sell people on the idea of low fixed interest rates, they tempted homebuyers with the idea they could get *even lower interest rates* by choosing adjustable rate mortgages as well as interest-only mortgages.

Meanwhile, there were two wars being waged, which were being paid for on credit. This disastrous debt lowered the value of the U.S. dollar abroad. The falling dollar meant that the United States had to pay for its oil abroad with more devalued currency. At the beginning of the Iraq War, oil sold for $25.00 a barrel, but those dollars were worth far more than the dollar is worth today.

The ups and downs of oil prices are, in an energy economy, another big factor driving our economic engine. Up until the summer of 2008, the price of oil was rising and people cut back on oil consumption. The price of oil immediately fell, revealing how much the spike in oil prices was not due to short supply but to speculation. Investors followed the money and moved away from buying up bad debt and into commodities. Then oil declined, and other commodities such as corn and wheat rose in cost. This dramatic rise in cost had a huge human cost in the starvation and near starvation of the poor around the world who live on the fringe and who depend on relatively stable prices for food to survive. Nobody who trades in commodities intends to starve the poor. Commodities traders are no better or worse than the average human being. It's not a matter of arguing over whether bankers or brokers or traders or anyone else are good or bad people. We have to think about humanity in general, and about the kinds of systems we create and why we do.

If we are only concerned about individual innocence or guilt, then we miss how many shortsighted and even morally wrong acts go together to create great disasters for many people. It is very important to remember that many of those making the decisions that created this huge mess are not themselves evil people. After all, what's wrong with stimulating the economy? Isn't it a good idea to help people buy a home who've never been able to afford one? Don't we owe it to our investors to make them a profit? Human beings are very creative and they will always think of new ways to do things, including new ways to make money. That's not always bad in itself.

This is why it is important to keep our moral reasoning in context. This is why it is important to see the connections between war and starvation, between easy credit and temptation, between individual sin and collective responsibility. It's too easy to think about sin and evil just as an individual. 'I'm not greedy,' you tell yourself. Yes, but together human beings are greedy and you are part of humanity whether you like it or not. Religious beliefs that focus only on the individual's moral life can be a big part of the battle over the innocence of the economy

HOW CONSERVATIVE CHRISTIANITY
HELPED AMERICA GO BROKE

Americans have had a lot of help in falling into temptation regarding the factors that drive the boom and bust cycles of the economy. Conservative Christianity has not only convinced people that there's a coming "Rapture" that will punish the guilty and reward the innocent, it has also applied this idea of the "saved" and the "damned" to the economy. This has fed the idea that markets are innocent and economic disaster is really the fault of those bad "sinners," in this case, not the rich, but the poor.

The strains of *The Battle Hymn of the Republic* conclude a *YouTube* video that appeared just as the extent of the damage to the U.S. economy was becoming clear. The video is called *Burning Down the House: What Caused Our Economic Crisis?*[8] Those who made this video cast the blame for the economic crisis on "bad government" and "social engineering" and, of course, Barack Obama.

This tricky slight of hand works this way: disconnected "facts" appear on the screen, one after another, pulsing rapidly for almost ten minutes. Then comes the pounding strains of "Mine eyes have seen the glory of the coming of the Lord." The video game speed of the "data" frames and the emotional appeal of the music are combined to keep viewers from realizing that the "facts" don't actually prove anything. "His truth is marching on!" is what everyone remembers from this abolitionist hymn. This video has been viewed more than two million times. *YouTube* viewers are helped to blame "government sponsored enterprises," and "low income borrowers" and even "bad social engineering" for creating the economic meltdown. The accusations of fault leveled by this video script are directed everywhere but at the systemic regulatory failures, the mortgage brokers, the underwriting firms, and the Wall Street speculators who actually *did* cause the subprime mess.[9]

Burning Down the House takes the "Rapture" idea of God's coming judgment and uses it to shift blame away from the real causes of economic catastrophe. This is surprisingly easy because, as was noted in the previous chapter, the idea that God is about to bash evil sinners for their many sins is widespread in popular culture and thus in American political life, as the sales figures for the "Rapture" novels attest.

The core concept stays the same whether applied to financial markets or attacking Iraq. The main idea is that there are sheep and goats, good people and evil people, the innocent and the guilty. It's a very useful and very adaptable idea. It's easy to understand ("we're good, *they're evil*) and it hooks people emotionally. Lots of frustrations and fears and uncertainties can be bundled up like political donations and packaged as religious righteousness. That's a very powerful political cocktail. The "we're good, *they're evil"* split of the Rapture (the bad'uns get *left behind*[10]) is extremely helpful to conservatives because it can be used to interpret lots of different kinds of historical events in religious terms.

As the economy worsened, the conservative theological view that there are good people who deserve financial success, and bad people who don't deserve our compassion got more and more traction. There are many good examples of the kind of blame shifting that took place, but one in particular was the rant of CNBC reporter Rick Santelli. Early on in the Obama presidency, his administration announced plans to pay the mortgages of people who had been paying regularly on their loans and then were in default because they'd lost their jobs. Santelli screamed that Obama's plan would just "subsidize the loser's mortgages." Santelli, of course, did not acknowledge his own possible complicity in some of the economic practices that lured people into bad mortgages.[11] "Losers" in a market-driven economy is just another way of saying "sinners." It must be your fault that the economy is not working for you, because the market is innocent. Only the guilty don't benefit.

WALL STREET 2

In Oliver Stone's 2010 film, *Wall Street: Money Never Sleeps,* the greedy Wall Street banker, Gordon Gekko, has seen the light. Gekko now knows that greed is not always good; it can lead to economic catastrophe. He partners with a young trader named Jacob, played by Shia LaBeouf, to warn the financial community of the coming economic disaster, and also to investigate the death of the young trader's mentor.

In the film, their warnings initially fall on deaf ears but then some people do wake up and smell the downturn. This is not so much the case in the real world, however. The warnings by critics of subprime practices went unheeded by those who could have done something to slow down the crash, if not stop it completely. But perhaps nothing could have pierced the bubble thinking. There is a profound conviction on the part of many that the market always works for the good and is thus innocent. In boom times, that idea is hard to refute.

For those who had eyes to see, an excellent example of warnings that came early and often about the financial risks we were running as a country came from a blog appropriately called *Eschaton*.[12] "Eschaton" is a theological word that means "the end of everything including the whole world." When theologians like myself teach religious beliefs about the end of the world, we call that part of theology "eschatology."

For "Atrios," the pseudonym for the blogger Duncan Bowen Black, signs of the end of everything as we know it are happening all around us, especially in our messed up political and social worlds. According to Black, the name *Eschaton* is a reference to an imaginary sport in the novel *Infinite Jest* (1996), as well as a word that is also used in the phrase "immanentize the eschaton." That means bring about the apocalypse. Just like the Rapture folks want to do. *Eschaton*, the weblog, is hugely popular and gets an average of 100,000 hits per day. But despite this high readership (for a blog) the architects of the subprime debacle went on their way, unheeding.

Eschaton is far more personal, sarcastic and "blogish" than some of the liberal blogs like *Daily Kos* or *Huffington Post* that now resemble online newspapers. Black (that is, Atrios) was one of the bloggers early on who tried to try to flag what was happening with the subprime debacle. Black certainly has the credentials to have read the financial signs of the times. He has a Ph.D. in economics from Brown University and has worked at the London School of Economics, the University of Southern California and most recently, Bryn Mawr College. He is also a Senior Fellow at the media research group, Media Matters for America. Other less theologically named blogs also sounded the alarm: *Angry Bear, Tbogg,* and *Naked Capitalism.*

An especially informative blog that was not so shrill and was based on facts, called *Calculated Risk,* specifically challenged the way that more mainstream journalists were *not* covering the coming subprime debacle. Their blogger, "Tantra," a pseudonym for a woman named Doris Dungey, shed considerable light on how home loans were actually made and what was going wrong in the whole system. Dungey knew what she was talking about. She had been a trainer and writer for such lenders as Champion Federal and AmerUs Mortgage. She also had the sarcastic blogspeak down pat. She wrote, in 2007, of Gretchen Morgenson, the *New York Times* financial writer, "I don't know how many posts I've written on Gretchen Morgenson's terrible reporting. I guess I'm going to have to start keeping score. 'Can These Mortgages Be Saved?' can this 'reporter' be saved?"[13] Dungey died of cancer in the fall of 2008.

Her "observations, with a hint of acid, helped the economics blog *Calculated Risk* become nationally popular. It gets more than 75,000 visits a day."[14] Thus, *The New York Times* noted Dungey's passing (though made no mention of her critiques of their reporter). *The Times* noted that Dungey's "fans" included Nobel laureate Paul Krugman who cited her on his own blog, and analysts at the Federal Reserve who included her work in a paper on "Understanding the Securitization of Subprime Mortgage Credit."[15]

It may very well be that the economist Robert Schiller is right and the "bubble" thinking that floated the idea that home values would continue to grow *ad infinitum* (until the end of times?) was unsinkable. The "bubble" thinking led many to believe what they wanted to believe, that the ever-expanding value of homes would be enough to carry any defaults on mortgages given to the A- to D borrowers (i.e., the "subprime" borrowers). Perhaps realism didn't have a chance. Bubble thinking is really just a modern way of saying "fall into temptation."

CAIN AND ABEL AS BANKERS

Many who run financial systems count on the fact that human beings are fallen, that they can be tempted and they believe what they want to believe. Very rarely, however, do some at the top of these financial institutions admit that they count on the collective frailty of human nature in order to do their business—even when it is becoming clearer they could take down the whole financial system. Every once in a while, however, they tip their hand and reveal that they do know that some financial schemes (not all) do rely on the fact that human beings can act in their own worst interest. Michael Lewis, former bond salesman for Salomon Brothers once flat out admitted that he and his traders relied on the fact that human beings are, well, human. He noted "The men on the trading floor may not have been to school, but they have Ph.D.s in man's ignorance."[16]

People aren't innocent and they often will their own ignorance when it is not convenient to see what the consequences of their actions might be. Human civilization with all its creativity about economics and technology, as well as all the other achievements of culture, is lived in the conflicts of Cain, not the innocence of Abel. Economic systems and the people who run them are not innocent—though they are not wholly depraved sinners either. Our economic system thrives on the desire of human beings for more, more of everything. This system has created great abundance, but it has also created massive suffering, loss, and even death from systemic inequalities, certainly many of them unintended, of this vast system. As the global economy has emerged, and as it has become "wired" through the Internet revolution, the ripples in the system are vast, they are global in scale whether for good or for ill. Eve's desire for more, and Cain's conflicts with his brother have gone global and innocence about the possible consequences of this is increasing our danger every day. Look out. The new "bubble" is already under construction—the time between boom and bust is decreasing, and without quick action to re-regulate the system in new ways, we're in for another economic "fall" very soon.[17]

FIVE

CREATION AND CLIMATE CHANGE

A huge velociraptor, one of the scary pack hunting, blood-thirsty dinosaurs made so famous by the *Jurassic Park* movies, calmly eats a pineapple. Two children, a boy and a girl, larger than life-size, play in a Garden of Eden paradise next to the fruit-chomping dinosaur. This imaginary Garden of Eden is the opening exhibit at the Creation Science museum in Petersburg, Kentucky. The vivid, animated scene is made possible through the magic of animatronics. It's a truly "wired" version of the innocence of The Garden of Eden played out in Disney-theme-park style. And it is powerful.

Mechanized puppets have been around for a long time. Who can forget the scary great white shark from *Jaws*? Animatronic people and animals, however, are more than mechanical puppets. Animatronic displays require sophisticated computer technology combined with engineering. The Walt Disney Company really pioneered this field, calling their inventors "imaginers." The "wired world" created at the Creation Science museum is a stunning example of how the creativity of the digital age can be used very effectively to help create a literal Garden of Eden "museum" and promote ignorance, not only about science, but also about religion.

The advertising for the museum claims it presents a return to biblical "literalism." The end game, however, is the sabotage of the political change needed to really deal with climate change. If "science" can be brought into disrepute by the rejection of Darwin and evolutionary theory, then the results of scientific documentation of the human activities that are accelerating climate change are also brought into question.

I visited the Creation Museum a few months after it opened. The brochure explains that "Children play and dinosaurs roam near Eden's rivers. The serpent coils cunningly in the Tree of the knowledge of Good and Evil... Enter the Cave of Sorrows and see the horrific effects of the Fall." As I entered the first exhibit and looked at the animatronic Eden, I wondered who these children could be, since the Bible does not say that Adam and Eve had children in the Garden of Eden. And, as we have been discussing, the children that are mentioned after they get ejected from Eden are two boys.

As I moved further into the Garden of Eden in the Creation Museum, I came upon Adam and Eve swimming decorously in a pool, Eve's hair arranged around her in post-fall modesty. Adam and Eve were not, of course, touching. In the Eden of this highly styled conservative version, all the dinosaurs were vegetarians and there was no sex. Sex and meat eating, the guidebook tells you, came about because of disobedience and the "fall" from the perfection of the Garden of Eden.

But the propaganda starts right as you drive up to the new Creation Museum. The first things visitors see are dinosaurs: dinosaurs on the signs at the entrance, dinosaurs as you approach the main museum hall, and especially the dinosaur playing happily with the children in the Garden of Eden. The big T. Rex, slavering jaws opening and closing through the museum's state-of-the-art animatronics, is called "our missionary lizard" for he (and she— the T. Rex family made it on to Noah's ark) is also vegetarian.

T. Rex is indeed a missionary because those who constructed this Creation Museum know this fact about kids: kids love dinosaurs. So, all the dinosaurs are missionaries to children and their parents in this 50,000 square foot museum dedicated to creationism. Kenneth Ham, President of Answers in Genesis—USA is clear, "We're putting the evolutionists on notice—we're taking the dinosaurs back."[1] Answers in Genesis—USA built the museum for $27 million. He echoes the attack war language that conservative religion uses to promote their cultural efforts at subverting science as an angelic/demonic struggle. Ham has set out to "Win the war of the world views," and young earth creationism is the tip of the iceberg that leads to all the other evils in our culture such as euthanasia, homosexuality and the breakup of the traditional family.[2]

Evolution has become a key cultural site for religious and political struggle in this country. "Creationism," the belief in a literal creation by God of everything in this world exactly as it is today, is also on the rise around the world. The most extreme of these views is the "Young Earth" movement represented by the Creation Museum—the earth, indeed the whole universe, they believe, is only 6,000 years old—a biblically derived number. "Old Earth" creationists have developed a website and program to combat the "Young Earth" creationists.[3]

Recently, some judges have found in favor of parents who have gone to court to prevent Creationism being taught as science in public schools.[4] Conservatives, recognizing this as a setback for their efforts, are now also taking the case for creation science directly to the people through museums such as the one in Kentucky. The www.creationism.org website lists twenty such museums nationwide, though the one that opened in May, 2007 in Kentucky is by far the largest and has the most sophisticated visual effects.

In his remarkable book *What's the Matter with Kansas?* Thomas Frank describes "how conservatives have won the heart of America. While leftists sit around congratulating themselves on their personal virtue, the right understands the central significance of movement building, and they have taken to the task with admirable diligence."[5] The mass movement work is paying off handsomely according to American opinion polls. According to a *Newsweek* poll (2007), nearly half (48 percent) of the American public rejects the scientific theory of evolution; one-third (34 percent) of college graduates say they accept the Biblical account of creation as fact. Seventy-three percent of Evangelical Protestants say they believe that God created humans in their present form within the last 10,000 years; 39 percent of non-Evangelical Protestants and 41 percent of Catholics agree with that view.

There are both extraordinarily cynical motives in those who promote the targeting of evolution as the motor of religious decay, and there are genuine and deeply held religious concerns. As especially well described by Frank, the cynical reason for conservatives bent on movement building to take up an issue like evolution is that it really cannot be resolved through concerted political action. The real reason to take up anti-evolutionary views as a conservative cause is to create a roiling distrust of liberalism. This generalized anger helps mobilize the conservative base and get enough votes for the real political agenda like letting polluters off the hook, gutting regulation, and cutting the budget of the Environmental Protection Agency. These are moves that are actually directly harmful rather than helpful to the material lives of that very same base.

There are also true believers among conservatives who are genuinely concerned about the capacity of the newer biological sciences to "play God" through gene therapy or other kinds of genetic engineering. The prospect of changing the human genetic code makes a lot of people very nervous. Could these scientists really change human nature? Conservative religion sees itself as the brake on a run-away, "mad science" that is bent on playing God. This anxiety about science then spills over and becomes a more wide-spread preoccupation with what is perceived as a general decline in morality in the dominant culture. Moral decline is represented by movies, television, video games, and music.

These believers have a genuine concern with the harmful effects of this dominant culture on the young, but they never look at the economic engine that drives the production of mass culture. Take the Fox Broadcasting Company, as an example. Its regular network programming consists of "reality" TV programs like *American Idol* that model cruel and cutting putdowns, sometimes even of the handicapped. They also have a slew of violent investigative dramas like *24*, as well as "cartoon" shows like *The Simpsons*, *Family Guy* and *King of the Hill,* which make fun of almost all the family values so beloved of conservatives. One show, *Dollhouse*, featured young women whose personalities have been "wiped clean" so they could be "imprinted to be a lover, an assassin, a corporate negotiator, or a best friend." The show was quickly cancelled, however. These programs, as they come and go, encourage the kind of "values wasteland" that American culture is becoming. And the Fox Network makes a lot of money from these kinds of programs.

But the main "news" programs on Fox News Cable network often feature pious rhetoric about "Christian values" and criticism of the supposed secularism of the left. Glenn Beck or Bill O'Reilly, two of the conservative social and political commentators for Fox, regularly tout conservative religious values and denounce cultural decline, while being paid by the people who make violent and degrading television programs. They are scarcely the only such conglomerates that promote "values" in one format, while actively subverting values in other formats, but Fox is particularly good at it.

The religious frame for the mass movement of conservatism keeps these economic connections from ever being made. Instead, the believer is preoccupied with the personal dimensions of salvation. The issue becomes the "truth" or "falsehood" of the Bible above all, and never who really profits from the kind of mind-numbing, values destroying junk our kids like to watch on TV. In the conservative view, the fault does not lie with corporations who know that violence and sex sell TV shows. Instead, the real culprit is *evolution*. It is evolution that is dragging down the morality of American society. The "literal truth" of the Bible in its description of the creation of human beings and the world is the only guarantor of morality and goodness. The polls cited above reveal the power and the polarity of this aspect of the culture wars; evolution is cast as an immoral secularism and literal views of creation are moral and faithful.

It is still very difficult for a new, less polarized and more dialogical American religion and culture to emerge because these distractions keep people from looking at the real issues that threaten our lives (in climate change effects) as well as our culture (in the junk that is now our cultural bread and butter, like "reality" shows). You cannot find real solutions to problems that are completely misidentified. Evolution is not the cause of a public culture of trash. Biblical literalism and creation museums will do nothing to really help us deal with new biological innovations and the kinds of ethical dilemmas they really pose. But in a wired world, there are increasing opportunities for distraction and for keeping people from making real connections.

WHAT'S THREATENING ABOUT
EVOLUTION?

Many religious people genuinely believe that Darwin's views about evolutionary theory are wholly incompatible with the idea that human beings are created in the image of God. After all, evolutionary biologists will argue that human beings are just random collections of cells on a randomly arranged planet in an impersonal and casual universe. This is a pretty grim view in the minds of many; certainly it's not inspiring for either religion or morality. Especially morality.

The biggest threat today that conservatives see in evolution is that it destroys personal morality. Religious conservatives have objected to evolution for a long time—in fact, from the time of Darwin. In Darwin's own time, his views on natural selection, in particular, seemed to undermine God's role as creator and sustainer of the world. Darwin's views were also used to support the "survival of the fittest" view of humanity, and that made them repugnant to the religious values of the time as well. In the nineteenth century, William Jennings Bryan, the famous Christian preacher, thundered against evolution in the famous Scopes "monkey trial." The Scopes trial was over whether a science teacher could teach evolution in a science class. But Bryan, who so strongly objected to the teaching of evolution, was not only concerned about science undermining the biblical view of creation, he was also concerned about the effects of what was called "social Darwinism." A century and a half ago, Darwinian evolutionary theory had been recruited in support of the brutal "dog-eat-dog" capitalism of the industrial age. Bryan hoped that in eradicating Darwin he could eradicate support for the brutal tactics of capitalist robber barons and make the country see the "evils" of capitalism run amok.

Today's religious conservative celebrates capitalism; there is no question of a critique of unregulated capitalism in their objections to Darwin's theories. The challenge today is to a kind of "personal" Darwinism where the primary threat is the teaching "that there is no meaning to life, no inherent value in humans and no absolute moral authority." A contemporary, anti-evolutionary website from "Creation Ministries International" quotes a "study" from Australia and argues that "moral decline is linked to belief in evolution," including "moral permissiveness," "premarital sex," "tolerance of abortion," and "divorce."

Evolution in conservative religious literature is cast as a "war against God" and all God stands for in terms of a personal morality that then affects public morality. Religious conservatives fear that evolutionary teaching in schools leads to "teen drug use, the rampant spread of sexually transmitted diseases, despair, and suicide in teens as well as youth violence."[6] While this can seem a tad extreme, it is the result of anxiety people feel when confronted by wave after wave of challenging scientific discoveries like the Human Genome Project. The HGP "mapped" the entire human genetic code, the pattern of chemicals that tell our cells what to do, and also pass on traits to our offspring, on high-powered computers.[7] The Human Genome Project has been called "The Book of Life."[8]

These scientific discoveries test the very beliefs people of faith hold about the origins of human life and the possible causes for human behavior. People of faith fear the consequences (whether valid or not) of the view that human beings are an integral part of the biology of the planet. This is a frightening view to many, especially when those fears are exaggerated for crass political ends. What are the young to do, asks the religious conservative, except fall into despair and self-medication when confronted with the idea that they are just a bunch of DNA with no moral purpose or meaning? I suspect that it is the adults, more than the young people, who are expressing their despair in this way.

The idea that evolutionary views cause moral decay comes from anxiety generated from the prospect that moral norms are not eternal and "God given" but simply natural impulses that change with every human whim. In addition, moral anxiety also arises when people are confronted with the prospect that human beings are just the products of natural selection and 'anything goes' with human nature as well. This is a very intimate and immediate threat to their self-understanding as human beings and their confidence in their infinite worth.

People who think the modern world, and especially modern science, is threatening their sense of God's control will turn to conservative religion as a defense. They seek the innocence of the Garden of Eden, this time taking the dinosaurs along, as seen in the Creation Museum. Their desire is for an all-powerful God who controls everything and who won't let anything bad happen to them or to the planet's biology through climate change. Yet, in their search for innocence and security they are actually working against the very things that could help all of us improve television shows, video games or films so that our young people can have uplifting entertainment options, and help all of us deal with the truly frightening changes to our world by actually engaging issues that threaten us, like climate change, rather than making them serve a politics of fear.

What would actually reduce the threat of climate change is better public policies that reign in the exploitive practices of businesses such as the oil and gas industries, and make sustainable energy and jobs a national priority. We are seeing an approaching dust bowl, punctuated by flooding in some midwestern areas of the United States. Other areas are experiencing better than average rainfall and longer growing seasons. These changing patterns are erratic and mostly damaging rather than beneficial. Parts of the country are becoming ecological and therefore economic catastrophes. Yet, fear of evolutionary theory keeps many people away from connecting the dots. They may complain about the increase in violent weather shifts, but resist relating those experiences to climate science data because they reject science as immoral. In the face of this disconnection, it is especially ironic that Darwinian evolutionary theory is still being used to justify rampant capitalism and it plays no part in informing the conservative religious *objections to evolution.* The reason is that the battle over evolution has moved from society to the soul. Yet, there are some conservative Christians who are trying to build bridges back to science in order to address climate change.

EVANGELICALS AND CLIMATE CHANGE

Some Christian liberals and progressives, as well as scientists, celebrated when a group of Evangelicals issued a statement in 2006 called "Climate Change: An Evangelical Call to Action."[9] This document was actually addressed to Congress and called for Congress to take action on climate change. The "Call to Action" distinguished itself from previous evangelical work on the creation in several ways. The first and most striking is the document's support of the fact that "human induced climate change is real" and the citation of scientific evidence to support this claim.[10] Second, the document points out the fact that the "consequences of climate change will be significant and will hit the poor the hardest."[11] The document sets its theological claim for the urgency of climate change action in the biblical view of God as creator, and that damaging the creation is "an offense against God himself."[12] But most especially, the document marks a break with the conservative perspective on government and business in its call for government and business to act together with churches and individuals.[13]

The statements on the economy and poverty are the strongest in this document, and open a door to a critique of capitalism. The document helps people see how capitalism itself has produced environmental destruction and human exploitation and how that is contrary to Christian faith. Combined with the use of scientific data and the appeal for a partnership among government, business, churches, and individuals, this document was a real departure for evangelicals on several levels, especially as it connects so many issues of faith, culture, science, and planetary care.

One of the architects of an evangelical approach to the environment is Richard Cizik who was formerly the Vice President for Governmental Affairs of the National Association of Evangelicals. In 2002, Cizik said that he heard a presentation on climate change and realized that this was a biblical, not just a political issue.

Cizik, along with Dr. Eric Chivian of Harvard Medical School (a prominent environmental scientist and founder and Director of the Center for Health and the Global Environment at HMS) co-hosted the launch of collaboration between scientists and evangelicals on health and the global environment. When Chivian was at the Massachusetts Institute of Technology, he helped start International Physicians for the Prevention of Nuclear War, which won the Nobel Peace Prize in 1985 for its efforts in highlighting the implications for global health of nuclear conflict. The participants in this effort produced a joint report from the medical school and the National Association of Evangelicals called "An

Urgent Call to Action" that built on the earlier efforts undertaken by evangelicals and called for urgent attention to human causes of climate change and the need for prompt public policy to address this concern. Cizik came under heavy criticism from religious conservatives, including James Dobson of *Focus on the Family,* for this initiative. In March 2007, Dobson and twenty-four other evangelical leaders signed a letter asking the NAE board "to ensure that Mr. Cizik faithfully represents the policies and commitments of the organization, including its defense of traditional values," and suggesting that Cizik resign "if he cannot be trusted to articulate the views of American evangelicals on environmental issues."[14] Cizik admitted to Bill Moyers that he did not add his name to the final draft of the report due to this kind of pressure.[15]

Richard Cizik once remarked to me and others at a meeting that he hoped the Creation Care initiative by Evangelicals would "build bridges" between evangelicals and scientists. Instead, the NEA backed away from Cizik, who resigned from his leadership position in the organization in late 2008, and by extension from this kind of collaboration with scientists on global warming. The reason that Cizik and the NEA parted ways was stated as the result of Cizik's changing position on civil unions for gay Americans.[16]

"Creation Care" per se has not gone away as an evangelical issue, though Evangelicals are stepping back from collaborating with the larger environmental movement especially when it comes to public policy, and stepping back from bridges with science. A Florida conference called "Flourish 09" called Evangelicals to a "new phase" on creation care "without the baggage." Flourish president and co-founder Rusty Pritchard was the first of many to declare, "I am not an environmentalist." This is odd, considering that Pritchard's career is as a natural resources economist who founded the environmental studies program at Emory University. Yet he considers that the term "environmentalist" is a "label...loaded with overtones of judgmentalism and apocalypticism."

Pritchard dearly wants to steer a course for his Flourish approach to the environment that runs between Sean Hannity on the right and Al Gore on the left. But in the middle, there can be no politics he argues. "Our engaging with environmental issues doesn't need to start with politics," said Pritchard. "That is the thesis of this conference. We have to start somewhere other than climate politics. There is nothing more divisive."

Mega church pastor Joel Hunter talked at the conference about how he worked creation care into the discipleship experience and stuck with Scripture to do it, avoiding "clever opinions" by which one would assume he meant scientific conclusions. In his article about Flourish 09, David Neff, editor of the Evangelical journal *Christianity Today*, shared his observation that "Evangelicals have often criticized the environmental movement for worshiping the creation rather than the Creator. At Flourish 09, there was not the slightest hint of nature mysticism. The dominant spiritual message was the need for neighbor love and the social justice activity neighbor love entails." And thus little science and less overt politics.

The Evangelical argument on Creation Care has a strong Christian theological argument to make about how human sin has damaged the creation and why Christians need to be concerned for the perverted systems in our global economy that create poverty and damage the environment. Evangelicals like Cizik who worked on building bridges with scientists on the globally catastrophic effects of climate change put theology together with science and with public policy.

Now, as seems to be the case in Flourish 09, the political implications of the policy changes needed to retard and reverse the effects of climate change, as well as the scientific evidence for human caused climate effects, are disappearing and being replaced with 'personal spirituality.' It is dangerously naïve to think that care for the creation can be accomplished without getting into either science or public policy. It is an imagined innocence that Richard Cizik, as well as some other Creation Care evangelicals, to their credit, saw from the beginning their work was bogus *from a theological perspective.*

The "Flourish" people are critical of what they call the "nature mysticism" of many in the environmental movement whom they feel have substituted an earth-centered spirituality for the worship of the transcendent God as conceived in Evangelical Christianity. Certainly some in the environmental movement do regard their care of the planet from a spiritual perspective, which is not at all similar to evangelical spirituality. The term "nature mysticism" does not describe all environmentalists, of course. There is evidence, however, that some in the environmental movement have a "back to the Garden of Eden" perspective that is just as risky for good public policy as is the "let's just keep our work on the environment in our churches" of the Flourish 09 evangelicals. It's just 180 degrees in the opposite direction.

THE GREENING OF EDEN: LIBERALS AND CLIMATE CHANGE

The liberal roots of the environmental movement are impeccable—and inextricable from the importance of Darwin's work. As with so much that defines the battle lines of our era, however, it was the 1960s when the environmental movement really took shape. Rachel Carson in her book *Silent Spring* (1962) showed the destructive impact of chemicals on the natural environment and predicted a coming environmental catastrophe. Earth First! is a radical environmental advocacy group formed in 1979 that claimed Carson's work as inspirational. Earth First! is movement oriented and rejects what organizers claim is the "sell-out" of mainstream environmentalism.

Earth First! illustrates one way in which the environmental movement is tempted to dream of Eden. On its website, Earth First! declares that one of its founding principles is "a belief in biocentrism, that life on the Earth comes first" along with their well-known practice of "putting our beliefs into action" including eco-terrorism as well as civil disobedience and lawsuits.[17] Earth First! is apparently committed to taking us back to the innocence of Eden (before Cain started making tools and planting crops), even if the rest of us don't particularly want to go.

Earth First! has been featured in the most popular of popular culture send-ups, *The Simpsons*. The episode "Lisa the Tree Hugger" features an environmentalist group called *Dirt First*, a parody of Earth First! The character Nick Van Owen in the film *The Lost World: Jurassic Park* reveals himself to be a member of Earth First!

"Earth Firsters" would be horrified by the following comparison, but with respect to their dreaming of Eden, they are not that different from the philosophy of Al Gore, except that Gore would, in fact, more likely respect an individual's right to choose whether they will be green or not. But Gore's faith in reason (*The Assault on Reason*) is such that he is convinced if you know the facts about climate change, you will choose to act in such a way as to prevent the worst of the pending climate catastrophe.

Al Gore turned a slide show into an Academy Award with his *An Inconvenient Truth* film and book. In the first pages of the book, Gore gives a classically liberal, Eden-dreaming pitch. A beautiful picture of the earth taken from space is accompanied by Gore's interpretation of the origin of the environmental movement. This picture, called "Earth Rise" was taken on an Apollo 8 mission. As the spacecraft emerged from radio silence behind the moon, Gore reports "the mission commander, Frank Borman, read from the book of Genesis, 'In the beginning, God created the Heavens and the Earth.'" Then one of the astronauts took the picture that became known as Earth Rise. "The image exploded into the consciousness of humankind. In fact, within two years of this photo being taken, the modern environmental movement was born. The Clean Air Act, Clean Water Act, National Environmental Policy Act, and the first Earth Day all came about within a few years of this picture being seen for the first time."[18] Thus Gore expresses his optimism that because humans know the good of planetary unity, they will work for the good of the planet. Gore himself seems to miss the point of his own example, however, as he works on building an environmental movement. It was the power of the image of Earth Rise as it raced around a wired world that brought about an increased consciousness of the beauty and fragility of the planet. Yet, most of the environmental leadership Gore and others provide is riddled with wonky scientific language that is abstract and distant to people.

Gore could not seem to leave well enough alone in his introduction. He should have quit after the Earth Rise image. But he doesn't, and the rest of the introduction serves as a reminder of the human capacity to sabotage even the best-intended solidarity in the service of saving the planet. Gore uses a quotation from well-known author, Archibald MacLeish, about the picture, Earth

Rise. The quotation itself reveals both the longing for human innocence and the kind of amazing blindness that are often the product of fallen humanity and its temptations to selfishness. Gore quotes MacLeash, "To see the Earth as it truly is, small and blue and beautiful in that eternal silence where it floats, is to see ourselves as riders on the Earth together, brothers on that bright loveliness in the eternal cold—brothers who know now that they are truly brothers."[19] Both Gore and MacLeash are, of course, completely and utterly blind to the fact that they must share this earth with sisters, mothers, wives, daughters, and all those who are *not* brothers. It is a statement staggering in its blindness and its pretence to universalism. And it is, sad to say, typically human.

The environmental movement is broad and extremely diverse. It includes radicals such as Earth First! and liberals such as Al Gore. It includes as well international and governmental agencies and an astonishing array of adherents in between. There are ecological and environmental scientists, conservationists, environmental health activists, nutritionists, and advocates for environmental justice to address the unequal impact of environmental degradation on racial/ethnic minorities and the poor. There are also the Gaia (earth is a living organism) believers, the deep ecologists, and now the self-described "bright green environmentalists" who emphasize good technology, design, and sustainable use of energy.

The longing for the "green" of Eden is scattered through this movement, and the methods used can be less effective for that reason. Just because people know the good, they will not necessarily do good. After all, Adam and Eve knew God's commandment in the Garden of Eden, *they just didn't do it*. Political, economic, and cultural strategies need to account for the fact that human beings are destroying the planet in part because humans are incapable of sustained innocence in their behavior. The "fall" from Eden is permanent and won't go away because we wish it so. The environmental movement has been losing credibility with the American public because it has not grabbed people emotionally, and made the case to them that their own self-interest is at stake in preventing further damage to the planet. Instead, the environmental movement uses scientific data, models of future events that are sometimes inaccurate (as modeling tends to be), and a version of shaming people for failing to be good, with calls to be good about protecting the environment. It's a strategy that's losing people.

Even cartoonists understand that people won't do things to save the planet just because you tell them they should. The talented creators of "Beavis and Butthead," "Office Space" and "Idiocracy" developed an animated sitcom called *The Goode Family* that ran through the 2009 season. *The Goode Family* tells about the lives of a family trying to live a "green" life. They have solar panels on their house, recycle "gray water" from their showers in order to water their plants, drive a hybrid car, and they are vegans. Their dog, "Che," is a vegan whether he wants to be or not and when he is unsupervised he tends to eat neighborhood animals and small pets, leading to a rash of "Have You Seen?" posters on the Goode's street. Their family motto is "What would Al Gore do?" plainly a reference to the Christian Evangelical motto, "What Would Jesus Do?"

The dilemma of the Goodes, and the point of the comedy, is that this sustained effort to be good in the conscious greening of their lives, does not make them fundamentally good. This was about as clear a portrayal of how it is *impossible* to get back to the innocence of Eden as you can get, especially in an animated TV sitcom. The conflicts the Goodes encounter in their 'good' lives are a pretty reliable guide to the fact that human life is lived after the fall from the Garden of Eden and there's no going back.

The premier of *The Goode Family* TV program may not have made environmentalists happy, but it made conservative columnist George Will ecstatic. He was so pleased, he wrote in a column, that the creators of *The Goode Family*, in his view, intended to blunt some of the "incessant hectoring by the media-political complex's 'consciousness-raising' campaign" that is designed, in Will's view, to badger conservatives like himself into being green. Finally, Will celebrates that there is some media comeuppance for those "planet-savers" and their "grating smugness."[20] Unfortunately, both for the show's creators and for Will, it was cancelled due to low ratings.

What would probably send George Will over the edge, not merely into print, is environmental apocalypticism. Like the conservative Christian apocalyptic on *The Rapture*, there are fictional depictions of the immediate end-of-the-world through rapid climate change. One such film, *The Day After Tomorrow* (2004) became one of the fifty highest-grossing films of all time. In this world-ending climate apocalypse, the catastrophic effects of climate change happen not over decades, but in just four to six weeks. Some scientists gather data proving that shifts are occurring in the ocean's currents that threaten an immediate return to the Ice Age. "Mr. Vice President, if we don't act now it's going to be too late!" yells the climate change scientist played by the lead actor, Dennis Quaid. "This is very urgent, sir. Our climate is changing violently, and it's going to happen in the next six to eight weeks." The vice president, however, growls and rejects the scientist's warning. The vice president in the movie bears more than a passing resemblance to then Vice-President Dick Cheney.

GREENER

We need to see Al Gore and Dick Cheney as the liberal versus the conservative "public theology" alternatives on climate change. Gore bores you to death and Cheney scares you to death. Both of these men represent temptation—they tempt you to see yourself as innocent and blame all your problems on the idiots who don't agree with you. Real goodness isn't innocent, and it doesn't blame others. Real goodness is the cultivation of wisdom about the fact that people really aren't innocent, and we have a lot of responsibility for our own problems. Real goodness is creative about options, and can still laugh at itself because it doesn't have all the answers. Real goodness doesn't scare you or bore you, it inspires you.

PART THREE

A Better Story

SIX

THE PRACTICE OF GOODNESS

An interesting aspect of the story of the Garden of Eden has to do with the snake. The snake was "crafty" enough to lie to Eve about the fact that if she ate the apple, she wouldn't die. That's where the expression "you lying snake" comes from. But in one respect, the snake *didn't lie.* The snake told Eve if she ate of the forbidden fruit, "your eyes will be opened, and you will be like God, knowing good and evil" (Genesis 3:5). That part is true.

One consequence of the fall, the expulsion of Adam and Eve from the Garden of Eden, is that people know good and evil. Unfortunately, just knowing good and evil does not mean that people always choose the good and shun the evil, despite what *The Goode Family* may believe. But knowledge is the big fruit that human beings gained in the Garden of Eden. This knowledge makes our lives a turmoil of creativity and destruction, cruelty and compassion, blindness and great insight. Just because we are no longer innocent doesn't mean we are wholly evil.

But we don't know everything. Even worse, at some level human beings know or at least suspect they don't know everything. This makes us insecure and prone to try to reassure ourselves that we do know what we're talking about and that we have the knowledge to control our world, and these days, especially our economy. We crave certainty, both in our own lives and in our institutions and our society. We demand certainty, and the more we feel uncertain and anxious, the more aggressively we pursue certainty. The lesson of Cain is that the way people deal with their insecurity about their existence is to pursue power, religious or secular (and oftentimes both together), in order to control the fear that *we really don't know what to do all the time.*

Conservative religion is very tempting to people because it gives them the comforting illusion that they are innocent and they can have the absolute knowledge of good and evil. Conservative religion's promise to people is that those religious leaders will tell us what to do and there is safety in that. They'll tell us who is who and what is what, clearly defining the lines between those who are good, and those who are not. They know who the saved people are, the innocent people, and they know who the damned are, the truly guilty folks. They know the absolute truth about the economy and about our society and even about other societies. They know God is on their side and His "invisible hand" is guiding the markets so that the engine of the economy will keep on producing, at least for the worthy people and that the United States as a "Christian nation" will always win wars. (Remember this is an otherworldly belief system and the reality of economic meltdown or lost wars do not enter in to the equation).

But human beings are *not* God. Religious leaders, no matter how spiritual they may be, are not God. Ordinary people and religious leaders alike have the knowledge of good and evil, but they are also fallen. They are not innocent. Nobody is innocent. Everybody's fallen. Nobody gets a pass on that. People are not perfect—only God is perfect. And when people delude themselves that they do know absolute good and absolute evil, all they're saying is that they are God. And that never turns out to be true.

People will persist in believing their absolute truths even when evidence piles up that what they believe cannot possibly be true. That's as true of the "Rapture" as a way to understand the future, in a religious example, as it is of believing in "Ponzi schemes" as a more secular example. If it seems too good to be true, it probably is too good to be true.

When Bernie Madoff, architect of the largest Ponzi scheme swindle ever, kept producing profits even in market downtimes, why didn't his investors ever ask themselves, "how can I keep making these terrific earnings that seem too good to be true?" Madoff bilked really smart people out of millions of dollars in a scheme that went on for years because he knew this fundamental fact about human nature. People really don't want to look too closely at what they don't really want to know. Temptation is real and never goes away in human life. That is really what the "fall" means. Yet, some people do manage to be good.

GOODNESS

I have been teaching a course called "Good and Evil" for decades. And every year the part on "good" gets longer. This is not because my students and I find "evil" any easier to understand, but rather because it becomes harder and harder to understand all the dimensions of goodness.

When we think of real "goodness" we tend to focus on the extraordinary individuals who have been good in the face of true evil. I once had the pleasure of having dinner with the man on whom the film *Hotel Rwanda* is based, Paul Rusesabagina. *Hotel Rwanda* is a 2004 historical drama about events during the Rwandan Genocide of 1994. Rusesabagina, played by Don

Cheadle, is a hotel manager who manages to save more than 1,000 refugees and his own family from being slaughtered during the genocide. He grants them shelter in the hotel where he is manager, the Hotel des Milles Collines.

This independent film had an initial limited release in theaters, but was nominated for multiple awards including Academy Awards for Best Actor, Best Supporting Actress, and Best Original Screenplay. The American Film Institute lists it as one of the 100 most inspirational movies of all time and it continues to be one of the most rented films on services such as Netflix.

At dinner, I asked Mr. Ruseabagina why he had done what he had. Why had he risked his life and the lives of his wife and children to save so many refugees? He said that as a hotel manager, he had been trained to try and make people feel comfortable. At first, sheltering people, even during the incredible carnage of the genocide unfolding around the hotel, he felt was just part of his job. Then, he said, he found that his ability to calm people down and get them to accept creative solutions to their problems was a big help in negotiating for the safety of the people in his hotel with the warring factions.

He impressed me as a person, certainly, but it struck me that he was telling me the simple truth. He was good at his job and he found himself extending his natural ability to do that work very well in an enormous conflict. It was a step-by-step account, as the film well portrays, of the practice of goodness. I also asked him why he thought that the situation in Rwanda had tipped over from civil strife into genocide. He replied, "the radio." I was certainly surprised. He said that for weeks prior to the outbreak of the mass killing of hundreds of thousands of Rwanda's Tutsis and moderate Hutus (the rival ethnic groups in the country) the radio blasted hate speeches, especially against the Tutsis. "They called them cockroaches," he said, and kept repeating they must be extermi-nated. This set the stage so that when Juvenal Habyarimana, the President of Rwanda, was assassinated, the pent up hatred trig-gered a vicious outbreak of violence. Over the course of approxi-mately 100 days, from the assassination of the president on April 6 until mid July, 500,000 people were killed. The final death toll was somewhere between 800,000 and 1,000,000. That is a killing spree of between 5,000 and 10,000 people per day over that period. Rwanda is a small country and today the population is just over ten million.

Saving anyone, let alone 1,000 people, from this spasm of vio-lence was extraordinary. But the example also shows ordinary goodness. The hotel manager was good at his job and he took that good practice and extended it, in spite of huge obstacles, to the warring factions. The negotiations, as portrayed in the film, illus-trate the ability of Rusesabaigna to find out what people needed and somehow supply it. The other point this example illustrates is that evil doesn't fall from the sky. It is created and often with very simple means, as, in this case, with radio broadcasts. Both good and evil are really quite ordinary. Goodness is the practice of goodness, it is not a spiritual possession that entitles you to succeed financially in this world as some conservative Christian leaders might lead you to believe.

THE PRACTICE OF GOODNESS

Even saints aren't good all the time. Mother Theresa admitted to lying about her own doubts and lived a double life for many years, outwardly confident in her faith and a model of saintliness, and inwardly wracked with doubt. But there is no question that Mother

Theresa did a lot of good. She provided care and compassion to many people society ignored, the poor, the sick, the orphaned, and the dying. At the time of her death, her Missionaries of Charity ran 610 missions in 123 countries.

Goodness is a practice, it is a cultivation of traits that tend to make both individuals and whole societies more capable of enhancing well-being and minimizing pain, suffering, and loss. It is important in these times, given the lack of well-being of not only human life, but also the life of the planet, that the idea of goodness as enhancing well-being be extended to the whole biosphere and not just confined to human life.

This notion of goodness fits with the idea that human beings fell "upward" from the Garden of Eden; that is, human beings are not created perfect and then become imperfect, so much as human beings are created immature and are learning. The "fall upward" interpretation being proposed in this book, however, is not that of an older liberalism where there is a nice, steady progress upward in human history toward enlightenment and thus greater goodness. That's when the "Goodes" and the "green" stereotype they represent go wrong. The struggle to be good in a fallen world never goes away. Progress on one hand is often accompanied by subversion on the other.

People are not innocent. People are human and as such are stuck between their natures as physical and spiritual, killers and creators. These are not diametrically opposed. As was discussed in the Cain and Abel chapter, even when human creativity leads to technological or social progress, some of this progress in turn creates the conditions for greater exploitation and alienation by some over others.

A practical approach to goodness takes into account that people aren't innocent angels. A practical approach that lays out a set of practices avoids the innocence trap, while also engaging the world as it is, not as we wish it to be. Good practices are those that lead to enhancing well-being and minimizing pain, suffering, and loss. This practical notion of goodness can be interpreted from different religious perspectives in different ways. It fits well with the needs of a religiously pluralistic society to be able to organize its economic life in a way that enhances human and planetary life. It also recognizes and takes account of the need to guard our economic life and our planet because of the profound imperfections in human nature.

PRACTICE NORMS

Creating a healthy economy is rather like creating peace. The key thing we need to be aware of is that healthy economies and peace don't just happen. Wishful thinking is not enough. Most people want peace and want the economy to be healthy for us and for the planet—but yet we have war and economic exploitation all the time.

Peace, or a healthy economy, or any other social improvements occur because we cultivate certain virtues that make them more likely to happen. Peace or a good economy happen not because we make an ideal model and then expect human beings, despite all evidence to the contrary, to stop being greedy or violent and just start being good. Utopian ideals were rightly ridiculed by Reinhold Niebuhr as not only being unrealistic, but downright dangerous because they are not connected to the way in which human beings act out of very mixed motives, and how human beings can be so blind to their real motives in the ways they act. In his "Christian realism" he cautioned us to be suspicious of the kind of idealism that ignored what really happens in human life.

During the 1990s, a group of twenty-three Christian scholars and activists argued about the problem of peace-making. I was one of them. We were all people who had worked on peace statements for several Protestant denominations and the American Catholic church. We wanted to write a joint peace statement and we almost quit because we couldn't decide whether what we wanted to do was make a list of abstract principles or ideals, or develop specific political strategies and give them religious support. We ended up not doing either. We worked out our conflicts because we chose a model we called "practice norms." Certain practices become normative for peace when they demonstrate, time after time in history, that more peace and less war results from doing these kinds of things. This approach finds a way to positively describe how peace comes about in both individual behaviors and *in social systems.* Realists warn us that people and nations have selfish interests and engage in power struggles and idealists warn that without principles we risk moral relativism. In terms of the story of Adam and Eve, we would say people are tempted to sin all the time. Yet in the midst of the national and individual self-interest and drive for security, the world is not always at war. In other words, some good happens. While principles can provide guidance, we need to check principles against the reality on the ground.

What is actually happening when violence is not occurring and people are living in peaceful relationships with their neighbors? What is happening to make that happen? Moral philosophers and theologians spend a lot of time working out abstract principles of peace, but in truth it is actually not all that difficult for individuals and nations to know the difference between peace and war, between destruction and creation, between threat and security. You know it when you live it.

What about climate change — Too late to the Party?

From these practice norms, this group of Christian scholars and activists was able to come up with a list of ten practices that increase peace and justice and decrease the likelihood of conflict, violence, and war.[1] We realized that when people and nations practiced conflict mediation, engaged in nonviolent direct action, worked for human rights, created real democracy, had just and sustainable economic systems, acknowledged responsibility, and sought repentance and change, and when they reduced weapons and the weapons trade and engaged in grassroots peacemaking, more peace and less violence had occurred in the world. So we described these practices as "just peace" and advocated that people do these things more routinely. In his Nobel Prize acceptance speech, President Obama mentioned Just War theory, but went on to say that it "is buckling" and that "what is required now is to think in new ways about the notions of Just War and the *imperatives of Just Peace*."[2] Currently, work is underway on a complete Interfaith Just Peace statement with Muslim, Christian, and Jewish scholars and activists.[3]

In the next section, "A Good Economy," we will look at a "practice norms" approach to making the economy work in a way that is realistic about human nature and the planet. But it is important to emphasize that the practices of good economics like making peace require that human beings learn things. We not only have to engage in good economic practices, *we have to practice being better people and better societies.* This doesn't mean being perfect, and it certainly doesn't mean being innocent. It just means cultivating some virtues we can practice that will help us work out an economy that does more good than harm. These virtues are different from the kinds of virtue that have resulted from a conservative religious viewpoint. Conservative religion divides people into the saved and the sinners, the innocent and the guilty. The saved deserve economic and political reward in this life and will be shot right up into heaven in the Rapture so they can have their reward in heaven too. The sinners, on the other hand, do not deserve economic or political equality in this life and they will be "left behind" literally (they don't get to have economic advancement) and spiritually (God will not save them from their sins at the end of history). This perspective is not adequate to the human story as a fall "upward" where everybody and the planet matter and should matter to everyone on the planet.

Having a healthy economy means cultivating the virtues that will encourage you to take other people into account. In addition, it means cultivating the virtue of seeing your self-interest clearly and the need to transcend that narrow self-interest not only for the sake of others, but in fact for your own sake as a person who can grow past the worst of human temptation to selfishness, jealousy, greed, and even violence. Falling upward means, in short, 'get over yourself' and realize how limited and even, yes, silly your tendency to be blind to your own self-interest can make you. A "public theology" way to do this is to learn to laugh at yourself and in laughing cultivate a little self-awareness and a little modesty in the face of the messy contradictions in all our lives.

CULTIVATE SELF-CONSCIOUSNESS

Did anybody laugh in the Garden of Eden? The Bible doesn't report that Adam, Eve, the snake, or God ever laughed. That's understandable. Perfection, on the whole, doesn't inspire a lot of humor. The fact that human beings aren't perfect, that they are "fallen" and can't get back to the Garden of Eden, has pretty much been a boon to comedians since Cain moved "east of Eden" and life after the "Fall" became the source of comic material. Comedy is very much a product of human imperfection, but it is surprisingly also one of the ways we can recognize how imperfect we are and learn to act to confront our foibles. Comedy makes you conscious of your own flaws in a way that doesn't totally turn you off. It is a practice of goodness because it helps people cultivate self-consciousness.

One of the ways American culture has been cultivating self-consciousness in recent years is through comedy. Comedy is rooted in the human capacity for self-transcendence. Comedy is one way we can actually see ourselves in all our stupid will-to-power stunts and our foolish grasping after a certainty that does not exist. We human beings are not only defined by our capacities for destruction and creativity. We also laugh. We are capable of making fun of ourselves, and of our own puffed up, self-importance, even the kind that leads to tragic consequences. Making fun of our own human temptation to overreach is a way to promote self-consciousness and self-transcendence. It's a way to remind ourselves we are not gods, we're really just human beings and human beings getting tripped up by our own pretensions to grandeur.[4] Increasing our capacity for self-transcendence is a key to becoming more decent human beings and having a more decent economy. When we can see our foibles and know our limitations, we are less prone to fall for the temptation of certainty. Comedy is not the only way to do this, but it has become an important way Americans have punctured some of their extreme self-delusions in recent years. If you want to resist temptation, tell a joke about yourself.

COMEDY AS A FORM OF
SELF-CONSCIOUSNESS

It is never recorded that Jesus laughed, though the Gospels do say that he cried. The Buddha, on the other hand, laughed all the time. In between these religious poles lies the truth of the human condition. There is plenty of cause for mourning in human life, but sometimes the best thing you can do to puncture you own inflated sense of self-worth is to laugh. Chris Rock, the brilliant comedian, commented in an interview about how he gets his comedy, like so many comedians do, from observing life and feeling its pain. "I hit my rough patches," he says. "Friend of mine, Rich Jeni, shot himself in the head...If somebody asks me, "Was he depressed?" He was a comedian!" He goes on, "A comedian is like half a psychic. Very aware. It is very, very aware to be a comedian. You kind of gotta notice everything....Stuff doesn't get by you...You just notice too much." The result of all this knowledge is comedy, and it's also pain. "It's so much easier to not know in life...You just end up knowing too much about people."[5] Jesus and the Buddha knew about good and evil—and that makes laughter and tears part of the same religious response.

On April Fools Day, 1991, the *Comedy Central* channel was launched. At first, this cable channel ran movie comedies and cartoon shows. In 1999, Jon Stewart took over *The Daily Show* and gave it a more political bent. The show received wide acclaim and a much wider viewing audience due to its coverage of the 2000 elections. With the invasion of Iraq, however, the *Daily Show with Jon Stewart* in particular became a source of criticism of this pre-emptive war and the nonexistent weapons of mass destruction when "embedded" journalists of the mainstream media were unable or unwilling to provide critiques. From "Rubble Without a

Cause" (04/08/03) to "Moment of Zen: Iraq Weapons" (01/27/04), several segments called "Farewell to Arms," in both 2003 and 2004, and Stephen Colbert's stinging piece "Non-Smoking Gun" (01/29/04), the show focused on the missing WMD's when they were not covered in the mainstream media. Stewart also repeatedly did segments on torture, including "Headline: A Few Bad Men" (05/04/04) and "Moment of Zen: Donald Rumsfeld" (05/06/04) when torture was under-reported, or misreported as just 'enhanced interrogation.'

In 2005, Comedy Central launched a *Daily Show* spin-off called *The Colbert Report* starring Stephen Colbert. This show was designed to ridicule personality driven political pundit news, especially those on Fox News such as *The O'Reilly Factor.* The key comedic theme of the show is that the anchorman (Colbert) is a poorly informed, right wing apologist who is very fond of his own views. Even the set of *The Colbert Report* enters into the comedic premise—there are huge American flags and the American bald eagle is the central icon on the desk. A running joke has to do with an American eagle named after Stephen Colbert.

Colbert is perhaps best known for his popularizing (and redefining) the term "truthiness," which dictionary publisher Merriam-Webster named its 2006 Word of the Year. As used by Colbert, the term is meant to lampoon claims of truth without regard to evidence, logic, critical thinking, or even facts. By using this redefined term, Colbert effectively lampooned the appeal to the "gut feeling" of contemporary political and social discourse. He particularly applied it to the decision of President Bush to invade Iraq in 2003. These comedy shows were enormously important for an American public mired in right-wing commentary as mainstream news (Fox) and fostered a critical distance, especially for young people, with news reporting in general.

The Comedy Central "fake news" shows draw a much younger audience than traditional news channels. In 2004, the Nielsen Media Research group put the average age of these viewers at 35. Young males between the ages of 18–35 view these comedy news shows more than all other news shows combined. A recent Pew Research Center survey (April 15, 2007) indicates that regular viewers of *The Daily Show* were more knowledgeable about the news in general than audiences of other news sources.

Comedy can help foster critical thinking and self-awareness. It can be especially effective in puncturing the balloon of overwhelming human self-confidence and inserting healthy doubt. Indeed, comedy can more effectively reveal the convoluted relationship between the human capacity to reach and create, and the human temptation to overreach and destroy. It sometimes does this far more effectively than straight-faced analytical articles or even books like this one.

John Oliver, a "reporter" on *The Daily Show* offered this revealing insight into the emotionally unstable amount of *uncertainty* in the country about the declining economy and protestations of certainty. "The amount of certainty you have is in inverse proportion to how stubborn you are and how angry you get," intoned Oliver in a segment called "Solving the Economic Crisis."[6] The point of the segment was that the crisis is insoluble and experts know it; hence, greater certainty is expressed! Oliver noted that the competing stimulus plans that were before Congress were regarded by the opposing party as having world-ending, apocalyptic results. According to Oliver, Republicans said not following their plan would be 'catastrophic,' while Democrats said that not following their plan would be 'Armageddon'! The economic crisis is a "dragon heading toward the castle." A film clip rolls of a press conference by Vice-President Joe Biden. "If we do everything right, and we do it with absolute certainty," says Biden, "there is still a 30 percent chance we'll get it wrong." The segment ends with a dragon appearing at the Biden press conference and spewing fire at the vice president, incinerating him. Now that's comedic insight into the reality that we're all scared about the economy and really don't know what to do about it!

Homer Simpson, and the entire town of Springfield as it has grown over the twenty years of the animated show *The Simpsons,* might not be regarded as a likely source of Americans waking up from innocence, but it has played a role. Somehow the writers of this long-running show have combined lowbrow humor that often features donuts into social satire, irony, parody, self-mockery, political commentary, and an unceasing send-up of television, particularly its home network. *The Simpsons* leaves no social problem un-lampooned including the risks of nuclear power, racial tensions, environmentalism, immigration issues and more. In fact, in the twentieth anniversary retrospective, the show opens with a new episode, "Once Upon a Time in Springfield" where preoccupation with the imminent demise of the world is ridiculed. Bart at a blackboard writes over and over, "The world may end in 2012, but this show won't." 2012 refers to the end-date of the Mayan calendar that 'end-of-the-world' predictors use as yet more 'evidence' that the apocalypse is about to occur. "Does Maya calendar predict 2012 apocalypse?" screamed a *USA Today* headline.[7] Now that's funny.

In the documentary that follows the new *Simpsons* episode, the writers have fun at their critics' expense. Now that the show is entering its twenty-first season, bloggers often gripe that *The Simpsons* used to be a lot funnier a decade ago, and boast that they've stopped watching new episodes. One of the current writers, Matt Warburton, says deadpan, "I think the Internet message boards used to be a lot funnier ten years ago, and I've sort of stopped reading their new posts."[8] It's a wired world dig, but an accurate one. Comedy in a digital world can be unfunny, and even cruel.

EMPATHY AND CRUELTY

Comedy does not always produce greater insight and lead to self-awareness. Sometimes, comedy is cruel and it can have the opposite effect, leading to anger and rejection. Cartoons seem an unlikely cause of international conflict, rioting, and death in some countries, but that has happened. In a wired world, cartoons from one country can travel all over the world in a matter of hours. In recent years, this is how some cartoons have played a surprisingly large role in national and international affairs.

The best known may be the worldwide controversy that began in September 2005 over twelve editorial cartoons published in a Danish newspaper, most of which portrayed the Islamic prophet Mohammad in various unflattering ways,. The debate caused the cartoons to be reprinted around the world, adding greater insult from a Muslim point of view, and furthering what has become an international crisis for Denmark. Critics have described the cartoons as designed to foster "Islamophobia" under the guise of humor. Supporters claim the publication of the cartoons is an issue of free speech and that unflattering cartoons about other religions are common in Danish newspapers.

Cartoons have been a popular way to ridicule President Barack Obama. Racist attitudes toward this first African American U.S. President are often disguised as comedy. For example, in early 2009, the *New York Post* published a cartoon that showed two

New York police officers who had just shot and killed a chimpanzee. The caption reads, "They'll have to find someone else to write the next stimulus bill." This was a clear reference to Obama, and in a context of fatal violence. It was also an attempt to deal with anxiety about the economy, but in a way that is opposite from the John Oliver segment. The *New York Post* cartoon is comedy as cruelty and it does not incite self-transcendence, but self-deception. This cartoon, and the many "cartoon" attacks on Obama through race feed the illusion that 'we don't really mean it' and it's 'just a joke.' But in truth, this kind of cruelty, disguised as comedy, serves only to give us permission not to identify with other people, and certainly not to care about them or feel empathy toward them.

TRUST AND NATIONAL GOODNESS

Empathy is in short supply in the United States, and empathy is crucial to cultivating trust. Trust is a practice of goodness; the beginning of a lack of trust in government, that is, trust that national goodness was even possible, began during the Vietnam War. Ironically, it is indeed the very idea of the goodness of the United States that starts us down the path to Vietnam. Henry Luce, born in China to Christian missionaries, was the influential editor of both *Time* and *Life* and in 1941 he captured the spirit that would carry the United States through WWII and lead us to war in Vietnam. In an editorial in *Life* magazine, Luce blended a kind of religious zeal, an astonishing conviction of American goodness and benign intentions, and mixed in the mandate to defend (and even extend) democracy:

> We need most of all to seek and to bring forth a vision of America as a world power, which is authentically American...America

as the dynamic center of ever-widening spheres of enterprise, America as the training center of the skilled servants of mankind, America as the Good Samaritan, really believing again that it is more blessed to give than to receive, and America as the powerhouse of the ideals of Freedom and Justice—out of these elements surely can be fashioned a vision of the twentieth century...the first great American century.[9]

Luce, faced with pointed criticism and even derision especially by Reinhold Niebuhr, actually recanted his editorial. Niebuhr inveighed against the "egoistic corruption" that comes to nations when they indulge such fantasies about their own goodness.

The American people were told they were going to war in Vietnam in order to spread "freedom and justice." Ultimately, however, deception about what was really happening there eroded the trust of the American people in government. This is what Rick Perlstein argues in *Nixonland,* "Lying about Vietnam" became "a Washington way of life."[10] There were no "fronts," no measurable progress, no allies, no clear objectives and finally, no winning hearts and minds. The reports of massacres such as Mi Lai dealt an agonizing blow to American self-understanding as spreading freedom and democracy. The reason we kept pouring personnel and money into a war was not, in fact, to spread the divine light of democracy. By the mid-1960s most people in public office, including the President, knew that Vietnam was hardly a country at all and its leadership was deeply corrupt. In 1965, Johnson justified another escalation this way: "We must fight if we are to live in a world where every country can shape its own destiny."[11] But in fact, "according to a memo filed by Assistant Secretary of Defense John McNaughton a month earlier, 70 percent of the reason we were fighting was 'to avoid a humiliating U.S. defeat.'

Helping the people of South Vietnam shape their own destiny he listed at 10 percent."[12]

Johnson, with his incredible political instincts, was also stuck, or thought he was. He thought "if I left that war and let the Communists take over South Vietnam, then I would be seen as a coward and my nation would be seen as an appeaser, and we would both find it impossible to accomplish anything for anybody anywhere on the entire globe."[13] Lying about the war in Vietnam, in Johnson's estimation, was the price for getting Civil Rights legislation through Congress. There's no question that good was accomplished through passing and enforcing those Civil Rights laws. But the casualties from the war in Vietnam were enormous, not only thousands of dead and wounded, but also our national unity and our trust in government (and institutions generally). The Johnson legacy in public policy is a textbook example of how good and evil are intertwined and that for every good, the capacity for destruction is there, tempting us.

AMERICAN GOODNESS

The "fracturing of America" is still a powerful legacy of the 1960s. "Fractured" is really a more accurate way of describing how the nation grapples with public policy than the more popular "culture wars" language. "Culture wars" describe certain hot button issues like abortion and homosexuality. Our "fractured" society is a broader description that includes the legacy of distrust of national institutions and the suspicion of science, for example. There is a widespread distrust among Americans that extends from Congress to Wall Street to Main Street and to your town and perhaps even into your own neighborhood.

Were we ever not fractured? As the film *Pleasantville* demonstrated, America in the 1950s was not really unified and harmonious. A surface conformity was achieved by repression of diversity. It is the surface conformity that was fractured when diverse groups demanded to be seen and heard in the public square. When groups who had been excluded from the cultural center demanded they be heard, groups such as African Americans or women, they could not simply be included without drastically changing culture itself. This destroyed whatever actual national unity existed and has not yet allowed us to embrace a genuine pluralism in our public debates. In the metaphor of *Pleasantville*, the upheavals of the 1960s added color, dimension, and most of all, a pluralistic notion of good and bad, right and wrong, innocence and guilt. But we have not yet embraced pluralism. In fact, many forces conspire to keep us from achieving a level of acceptance of diversity and an honest give-and-take that is a requisite for a good society to function and deliver for its people. The turmoil of the 1960s, not only in regard to race and gender, but also the wrenching national catastrophe that the Vietnam War became, is a wound in the American psyche that is continually prodded and never really heals. Americans may tell pollsters that they want "bi-partisanship," but then fail to support efforts to achieve it in such crucial national issues as health care. The enormous amount of money that comes from lobbyists is, of course, one of the main reasons Americans can be so easily fractured and re-fractured and set at one another's throats, even over issues like a public option on health care that early on in the health care debate, 70 percent of the public said they supported.

It is not always conservatives on the Right who reject trying to heal the fractures of our society and find a way to practice goodness in politics. An example from the Left is the hysterical rejection by people who hold different positions on the abortion debate to find "common ground." 'Being a centrist' is an insult for both the far Right and the far Left. Betrayal lurks beneath every policy consideration.

Self-awareness and cultivating trust in one another, however, are practices of goodness because they actually produce social power. They produce social power because they increase our capacity to work together even across divisions of political ideology or religious belief, or both. The "fracturing" of America is producing another kind of power, the power that comes from fear and that shows itself as aggression and the will to domination. The ultimate risk of this kind of extreme polarizing power is that, at the end of the day, we will end up alone because literally no one agrees with anyone else 100 percent of the time.

SEVEN

NATIONAL SECURITY: WISDOM WITHOUT INNOCENCE

President Obama was wise to show restraint in his rhetoric regarding the unrest in Iran following that country's apparently rigged presidential election. American conservatives, however, convinced as they are of the innocence of American power and our "support for freedom" around the world, called him "weak" and "indecisive." They simply could not seem to accept the fact that American power is not innocent, and that President Obama expressing support for the protestors in Iran would have helped the oppressive Iranian regime portray them as American puppets and therefore traitors.

It was a test case for Americans on how we can be smarter about national security when we give up pretensions to American innocence. It was telling that President Obama had to explain himself to the American people for not throwing American power in the face of an oppressive regime and thus create a backlash against the protestors. America's security in the future will depend on how much we are able to give up dreams of America as innocent, and accept that we can be wise without illusions about our power. And, of course, President Obama was aware, as many of his critics were not, that the true end game with Iran is nuclear.

PUTTING THE ATOM BACK
TOGETHER AGAIN

When President Obama gave a speech calling for the eventual elimination of nuclear weapons, critics said he was indulging in "fantasy." Others, like Joe Cirincione of the Ploughshares Fund, a foundation focused on nuclear weapons and conflict resolution, said the elimination of these weapons was not fantasy, but "the new realism."[1] Some observers quoted President Ronald Reagan who had also said, "We seek the total elimination of nuclear weapons from the face of the earth."[2]

So which is it? Can we realistically eliminate nuclear weapons or is this just the liberals indulging in wishful thinking? (Except, of course, nobody thinks Ronald Reagan was a liberal.) The reality is that the world has already made tremendous progress in nuclear weapons reduction, and steps toward their eventual elimination are underway. In fact, the gradual elimination of nuclear weapons is one of the great success stories in international diplomacy. Far from being a fantasy, the slow and steady progress on nuclear weapons reduction, the prevention of more nuclear-armed states, the elimination of atmospheric testing of nuclear weapons, and the near elimination of underground testing has been going on for decades.

Citizens organized "Ban the Bomb" protests in the 1950s—this activism gave rise to the actions by Presidents Eisenhower and Kennedy to halt atmospheric testing unilaterally. When the Soviet Union followed suit, the Partial Test Ban Treaty of 1963 was the result. Later, Soviet President Gorbachev and President Bush senior managed to achieve dramatic reductions in nuclear arsenals. In the 1980s, the very successful Nuclear Freeze campaign achieved a number of significant reductions in nuclear weapons systems, especially in slashing funding for the "Stars Wars" program that would have re-escalated the nuclear arms race. There have been decades of painstaking and effective measures to control fissionable materials, prevent non-nuclear states from acquiring nuclear weapons, getting nuclear states to give up their weapons, and to work toward "nuclear free" regions of the world.[3] As recently as the 2009 stimulus bill, non-governmental groups were able to pressure Congress to eliminate a billion dollars from that bill for funding nuclear weapons.

In the 1950s, however, many people thought that the world would see not one but several nuclear wars before the end of the century—the nuclear arms race was on. The early 1960s were a time of escalating tensions between the Soviet Union and the United States—the Berlin Wall was built in late 1961. The world probably came closest to nuclear war in what is called the Cuban Missile Crisis in the fall of 1962. But the diplomacy worked and the ships carrying the Russian missiles turned back from Cuba. Vietnam, a bloody, "hot" war of the Cold War escalated with direct U.S. involvement in 1965 and didn't end until 1975. Recently declassified documents show that in his first year as president, Richard Nixon considered using nuclear weapons in Vietnam.[4] We did not get into a nuclear war with Russia over Cuba. Nuclear weapons were not used in the Vietnam War. That's the reality.

But the threat of nuclear destruction worked on the American psyche, especially during the 1960s and then again post 9/11 (see Chapter 1). Movies are a great way to peek into what is going on in the American subconscious. In the 1960s the idea that nuclear war would occur was lurking in the American psyche and Hollywood produced a lot of films that spoke to this often unspoken fear.

The 1968 film, *Planet of the Apes,* reveals our fears of a post-nuclear holocaust world. *Planet of the Apes* is also a retelling of the story of the Garden of Eden. Charlton Heston stars in the film and plays one of a small group of astronauts who have been in deep space hibernation. They crash land on a planet that they think is light years from earth. This planet is ruled by a society of talking apes who subjugate and even try to exterminate every human they can find. The surviving astronauts are captured by the apes and imprisoned. Ape scientists who study them are astonished when they discover that Heston, though a human, can talk. The leader of the ape society does everything he can to destroy that knowledge.

Rod Serling, the famous science fiction writer best known to Americans as the creator of the TV show, *The Twilight Zone*, co-wrote the screenplay of the first *Planet of the Apes* film. Serling is credited with the dramatic post-nuclear ending of the film. Heston's character escapes from the apes with a female human and rides off down a beach. Out of the surf, a partially destroyed Statue of Liberty rises. Heston realizes he is on earth in the future, an earth that had been destroyed in nuclear war. "You blew it up! Damn you...damn you all to hell! You did it!" he screams. Now Heston knows why apes rule earth, and why the ape society is so determined to keep humans subjugated and ignorant. The film's judgment is that human knowledge of nuclear weapons is too dangerous for the world and humans must be suppressed.

In *Planet of the Apes*, the Garden of Eden story is turned on its evolutionary head. In the Bible, human beings "fell" from the innocence of the Garden of Eden because they wanted to know more than was good for them. In the Hollywood fantasy, that knowledge was used for the near destruction of the planet and evolution reversed itself. Apes, the next step down on the evolutionary ladder, take over from the human beings who are too dangerous to be allowed to develop their scientific and technological abilities again. There can be no freedom on the ape's planet because freedom leads to greater knowledge and greater knowledge has been used for the destruction of what humans have achieved.

Planet of the Apes is a Garden of Eden story because the film suggests that it is knowledge itself that poses the greatest risk to planetary annihilation. The reason *Planet of the Apes* is a fantasy is that human beings have not been so destructive in nature that they have engaged in nuclear war. In reality, human beings are both creative and destructive. But it is true that we do not live in the innocence of the Garden of Eden.

There is a critical lesson to be learned from a new interpretation of the Garden of Eden narrative when it comes to the "elimination" of nuclear weapons. The weapons themselves can be eliminated. The history of non-proliferation, treaties, and actual weapons reduction shows that can be a real outcome. But what can never be eliminated is knowledge. 'All the king's horses and all the king's men cannot put the atom together again.' The knowledge of splitting the atom and the power for destruction that knowledge entails is just part of human history now in a way that it was not before the success of the Manhattan Project, the project that produced the first nuclear bombs. People now know how to do this; the innocence of a pre-nuclear world is no longer possible. J. Robert Oppenheimer, the bomb maker and philosopher who worked on the first atomic bomb, said of himself and his colleagues that "physicists have known sin; and this is a knowledge which they cannot lose."[5] But that does not mean that the lesson of the new Garden of Eden story is that human beings are only sinners and they only know how to destroy.

The doomsday scenario of repeated nuclear war, widespread fallout, and even nuclear winter has not taken place; in fact, since the first atomic bombs exploded over Hiroshima and Nagasaki, human beings have been working together creatively to limit the threat from these awful weapons. When human beings "fell" from the innocence of the Garden, they fell into the knowledge of *both* good and evil.

But new challenges arise every day. Where the former "mutually assured destruction" of nuclear deterrence served the purpose of pushing nation-states back from the use of nuclear weapons (because their own country would not survive it), that strategy is useless when the main threat comes from non-state actors such as terrorist groups acquiring nuclear weapons. When the risk arises of nuclear-armed states "failing," then there is a real, increased likelihood that non-state actors could acquire nuclear weapons. In addition, radical regimes could take over nuclear states and then arm terrorist groups. These risks are real and they remain.

POWER AND SECURITY

Wouldn't it be great if we could wave a magic wand and have the power to just eliminate all this risk and threat? Young adults who have grown up with the *Harry Potter* series of books know differently. One of the great themes of this extraordinary series is that there is no such thing as innocent power and that good and evil are remarkably intertwined.

For my generation, there was the powerful influence of the first *Star Wars* trilogy. *Star Wars* projects a truly innocent view of the world. There's the "Dark Side" (all bad things) and the Force (the power for good). The Alliance, who fight the Empire and the Dark Side, are good and true—Luke learns to use the power of the Force and he defeats the Emperor along with his stalwart friends. Peace and justice reign.

Just in case you have been living on Mars for the last decade, the idea of the J.K. Rowling books is not of a "galaxy far, far away" but of a clandestine and parallel wizard society that is alongside of and sometimes intersects with human society of today. The seven Potter books follow three children who grow up and go to school learning to be witches and wizards and who must confront and engage an evil presence that threatens them and their world.[6]

These books have been credited with increasing the percentage of people who read, especially younger boys. Is the Harry Potter generation also the millennial generation? They do overlap.[7] The first Harry Potter book, *Harry Potter and the Sorcerer's Stone*, was published in 1997. Potter readers have grown up along with Harry and reading has increased along with the Potter readers. Young adults show the most rapid increases in literary reading. Since 2002, 18–24-year-olds have seen the largest increase (9 percent) in literary reading, and the most rapid rate of increase (21 percent). This jump reversed a 20 percent rate of decline in the 2002 survey, the steepest rate of decline since the NEA survey began.

The widespread readership of the Harry Potter books has been a cause for celebration by some, but a cause for tremendous alarm for others. The Rowling series has been intensely controversial in religion, especially in the United States. Religious conservatives in the United States have objected to the series, often to the point of working to get the books banned from use in schools, because they "teach witchcraft." There has also been an outcry by the Christian right because the young protagonists, Harry and his two friends, sometimes lie or steal in their fight with their arch villain, Lord Voldemort and his magical minions. This struggle, like many other skirmishes in the culture wars, reveals the deep divide in how we regard education and the role of imagination in the development of an educated human being.

The conflict over the Potter books and movies also reveals a deep division in how we regard religion and its purpose and meaning in our lives. On one side of this divide is an understanding of religion as primarily fixed and rigid; religious education in this sense is memorizing doctrine and rules and applying them directly and without question in your (and your family's) life. Morality in this view is fixed and clear. On the other side of the divide stands an understanding of religion as a life lived in the struggle to understand this world and to find transcendent meaning in the midst of conflict, sorrow, loss, and death as well as in achievement, joy, and community. In this latter view of religion, the development of a moral sense is a deep engagement with the conflicting demands on human beings and the choices we make as we try to be accountable and responsible to a higher purpose.

The constant theme of the Harry Potter books is the illusion of total security in the real world. We are most at risk when we are wilfully blind to what's actually going on, and when we bury our heads in the sand and think we can do nothing to deal with risk and threat. J. K. Rowling herself has observed that it is "blindingly obvious" that the moral lesson of the books is the development of the sense in children, and the adults with whom they live and study, of the complex moral universe in which we live, the importance of resisting tyranny and the refusal to take the easy way out.

This is at the heart of religious maturity—the letting go of innocence and its naïve conviction that good and evil are simple and obvious. Children and the adults they become have to learn that the world is not perfect and that goodness is not always rewarded. Evil is a real presence in the world. Children can feel very powerless when, for example, they have a teacher who seems to be especially harsh. Children can have a hard time sorting this out, because authority figures like teachers are supposed to be good. Most teachers are trying to do their best, but some can be needlessly harsh and cruel (as can some parents, of course). When faced with such contradictions, children can truly feel helpless and abandoned.

The Potter books help both children and adults realize that there is good and evil in this world and you should not remain passive in the face of cruelty. In the age of the Internet, kids are subjected to cyberspace teasing and threats that make children's problems with bad teachers pale by comparison. The teachers and parents in the Potter books are also imperfect and not always right, but the good ones *are on the side of the children and the bad ones are not.* This is a critical lesson about community and how values are sustained despite the machinations of the wicked.

Rowling has written a series of books that have grown in complexity and maturity along with her readers. The last book, *The Deathly Hollows*, has racial prejudice as a major theme. Muggles (humans) are persecuted by the evil Lord Voldemort regime for being "mudbloods" and wizards and witches born into human families are contemptuously referred to as "half-bloods" (a theme of Book 6 as well). Muggles, and those who cannot prove their "pure-blood," are subject to registration, confiscation of property, arrest, and incarceration in concentration camps and even torture.

Torture is a prominent and difficult theme of the last book. The first chapter's central event is the torture and death of a former teacher at the Hogwarts School of Witchcraft and Wizardry. It is clear that Rowling wanted to make a strong statement about the fact that torture is always a sign of consummate evil.

Another striking theme of the Potter books is that of death. The villain's name, Lord Voldemort, means the wish for death.

Good people die in the Potter books, both young and old. The wicked also die, but often are able to subvert plans to incarcerate or even kill them. No one who has grown up in the late twentieth and early twenty-first centuries is insulated from the violence of war, murder, kidnapping, and a host of other threats to life and limb, both real and fictional. Compared to an average weekday night at 7:00 pm on TV, the violence of the Potter books can seem tame (though Book 7 is very violent), but all the same the books present the reality of violence because neither the adults nor the children can ever be totally secure and free from the threat of violence.

Magic isn't real, but even if it were, Rowling seems to be saying, it wouldn't solve anything because the only way problems are solved in the real world is through the strength of love, the bonds of human friendship and moral community, and the capacity and willingness to take action in the face of what is wrong.

SCARED STUPID

Why does humanity continually have to learn these simple truths about the practice of goodness? That's another one of the realities of human life and history that doesn't have an easy or simple answer. I have no idea why the great moral insights of the past get lost or even stolen and warped in later generations. But it happens. Contrary to what classical liberals think, history is not one long story of humanity's upward march to greater moral insight. There are a lot of setbacks. Of course, neither is history the pitched and violent battle between good and evil that conservatives think either. History is learning and re-learning how human beings can actually be decent to each other.

Practical goodness can be learned, but it can also be unlearned. What many of us thought had been settled once and for all in terms of what is morally right or wrong can again be brought into question only a couple of generations later. Most people thought that after the concentration camps of Nazi Germany were liberated and the horrors there exposed, that "never again" would really be "never again." Who would have thought that torture was not a settled moral issue? Certainly no one would have thought it wasn't a settled moral issue in the United States, the country that has been honored with the responsibility to preserve the original copies of the Geneva Convention. Who would have thought, after the Nuremberg Trials, that 'the lawyers said it was okay' would be offered as a reason why an American secretary of defense, a secretary of state, a vice president and even the president himself seemed to think that it was okay to torture just so they got some lawyers to say so?

The reason we forgot all those moral insights is our weak and fearful understanding of security. A new administration, charged with maintaining "national security," failed spectacularly to keep the country safe from attack by a few radicals armed with box cutters on 9/11. That administration panicked and in that panic they decided a response of brutality was the definition of security. They abandoned the rule of law, including one of the oldest rules of law, habeas corpus, in Latin "you shall have the body" or, in practice, have some proof. They held people without charges, without access to lawyers, without trial—in fact, without most of the rights outlined in the Magna Carta in 1215, especially prohibition against unlawful imprisonment. Why? Because they gave them a new title, "enemy combatants" and defined them as people without human rights of any kind. And so they could also be tortured.

A good case can be made that Americans have become morally stupid in the last decade. The fact that there has even been a "debate" about torture illustrates this. Everybody used to know that it was wrong to torture people.

What is "wrong" with torture is that it is purely designed to inflict pain. Torture can't be justified as a way to interrogate people in order to find out anything of truth. People who are tortured will say anything to make it stop, so torture is the direct opposite of truth. That's what makes it not only wrong, but morally stupid. This is the point Elaine Scarry so brilliantly argues in her book *The Body in Pain: The Making and Unmaking of the World.* An example Scarry uses, and a good example because most people can relate to it, is when a dentist's drill accidentally hits a nerve in a tooth and the patient "sees stars." What that simply means is that everything else in life: memory, experiences, and your whole being is obliterated and you become reduced to that "world-destroying" pain.

That's torture. And that's why torture and interrogation can have no true relationship. The only truth is the pain. Interrogation is a fiction of power, a power so unsure of itself that it can only lash out, not in investigation, but in revenge.

The absolute and incontestable truth of human pain reveals the society that authorizes its systematic administration as being scared stupid. Scarry says that torture is employed by political regimes to illustrate a "spectacle of power." What actually happens, however, is that the regime that employs torture is thereby revealed as "so unstable, that they use torture." In other words, torture as systematic brutality is supposed to look like power, but that is fiction. What is really revealed is that when a political power feels it has to resort to torture in order to exercise power, it is actually doing so because it is weak and unstable. This kind of political power is really a hall of mirrors, a fun house distortion of genuine political power based on democratic values.

The "torture apologists" from the Bush administration such as Dick Cheney have tried to argue that their policy of torture was "justified" because it "kept America safe." This is an extension of the moral stupidity—how stupid it is to think that you can cobble together a morality from acts so brutal that they are guaranteed to obliterate the truth of any information obtained? How morally stupid is it to refuse to see that this brutality created enemies for the United States instead of making us safer?

Real security only comes from strength and confidence in values. Real security is a process, a laborious process of building connections, working to reduce conflict and the reasons conflicts develop, reducing weapons and the weapons trade, increasing economic prosperity among the poorest peoples and nations, and increasing the rule of law, providing infrastructure—in short, practicing security that can be sustained.

SMARTER POWER?

Let's just assume that we were actually scared stupid in the last decade, stupid enough to think that security can only be attained through what is called "hard power," that is the kind of power that comes from the barrel of a gun, a tank, a missile, an army, or torture. "Soft power" is an alternative. "Smart power" is the idea that you can combine "soft" and "hard" power and be smart about what you use and when.

Joseph S. Nye, Professor of International Relations at Harvard University in 1990, first defined "soft power." It's often been mis-understood, Nye says, and yet in the age of terrorism it has never been a more appropriate understanding of power. Power's not that difficult to understand, Nye observes. "Power is the ability to alter the behavior of others to get what you want. There are basically three ways to do that: coercion (sticks), payments (carrots), and attraction (soft power)."[8]

British historian Niall Ferguson describes soft power as "nontraditional forces such as cultural and commercial goods" and then just dismisses soft power for being, "well, soft." Using hard power, or military force, doesn't mean that people will just do what you want them to do. People fight back. America lost in Vietnam despite the fact that we had more "hard power," including nuclear weapons, than anybody else. We're losing in Afghanistan for the same reason and it is not at all certain that the long-term verdict on Iraq will be that we will have Iraq as an ally and not an enemy.

In the debates over attacking Iraq, opponents of the war brought up the historic religious conflicts between the Shiite and Sunni in Islam, but those concerns were brushed aside as irrelevant. Democracy building, the previous administration believed, was more powerful than historic religious conflicts. Despite the fact that the Christian faith was a strong part of both the rhetoric and the worldview of the previous administration, it still obviously did not take religious factors seriously in foreign policy concerns.

The policy community in the current administration accepts cultural goods as attractive and a crucial aspect of power in foreign relations. Yet, religion is still often not seen as an important aspect of culture and an important factor in "soft power."

"Soft power" as defined by Nye, is the power of "attraction" as opposed to "coercion" or even "payment." It is not exclusively cultural power, but it does offer a greater range of options than force or coercion alone. Hillary Clinton, the Secretary of State-designate, in her opening statement at her confirmation hearing before the Senate Foreign Relations Committee, said, "We must use what has been called smart power, the full range of tools at our disposal—diplomatic, economic, military, political, legal, and cultural—picking the right tool, or combination of tools, for each situation. With smart power, diplomacy will always be at the vanguard of our foreign policy."[9]

Smart and wise are not always synonyms, however. For "smart power" to become wisdom in regard to national security, the power of religious factors in culture must not only be seen, but engaged creatively.

A SOFT POWER APPROACH TO
NUCLEAR PROLIFERATION

In the spring of 2005, a group of Muslim and Christian religious leaders and scholars met in New York in advance of the United Nations Nuclear Non-Proliferation Treaty Review Conference. This group was composed of equal numbers from each faith and representing the diversity within each faith. The Islamic Society of North America, the Managing the Atom Project of the Kennedy School of Government of Harvard University and the Rockefeller Brothers Fund, sponsored the meeting.

At the beginning of the meeting, it was not clear that this group would be able to produce a joint statement. Some of the Christians had worked together before on developing the Just Peace paradigm, but most of the interfaith participants were strangers. Yet, by the end, a consensus document was produced called "We Affirm Our Belief in the One God: A Statement Regarding

Muslim-Christian Perspectives on the Nuclear Weapons Danger," which has received thousands of signatures.

The breakthrough for the participants was to focus on the doctrine of God. Coming together around the shared religious conviction that God is the "Creator and sustainer of the universe," the group was able to articulate an anti-nuclear statement that was strongly worded and that unambiguously opposed "any weakening of the Nuclear Non-Proliferation Treaty."

The document called for the complete elimination of nuclear weapons, a position President Obama has recently advocated and that Joe Ciricione of the Ploughshares Fund has called "the only true realism." The statement also addressed non-state actors and nuclear terrorism.

> We further agree that the possession of nuclear weapons is an unacceptable risk for the human community in these times and is a continuing threat to the entire planet and its fragile ecosystem. The risk of theft of nuclear weapons or materials by non-state actors for nuclear terrorism as well as the continuing risk of accidental use of nuclear weapons by nation states themselves makes even the possession of nuclear weapons a danger to God's creation.

As a participant in the conference and one of the drafters of the statement, I was still amazed at how when we started out trying to 'get the religion out of the way' we were stalemated (yes, even religious leaders can go down that path, especially in interfaith contexts); when we sought to frame the argument in terms of our deepest and most meaningful religious convictions, we moved forward very rapidly.

From a soft power perspective, we must make a specifically religious argument part of the way we approach the control and eventual elimination of nuclear weapons. This approach deprives both states and non-state actors of a legitimate claim to a religious justification for the use of these weapons. Those who wish to perpetrate nuclear terrorism are already busy seeding their religious justifications for the possession and even use of nuclear weapons as God's will. It is only smart to counter them with soft power in the unambiguous statement that these weapons are *contrary to God's will* in both Islam and Christianity.

Muslims and Christians working together to provide a positive, religious grounding for the stewardship of the earth and thus a religious interdiction against the use of nuclear weapons is one example of how religious leaders themselves are working to have religion become an asset from a soft power perspective.

Preemptive theological work on nuclear weapons is not naïve, it is smart because it subverts the arguments that terrorists might use to acquire and use nuclear weapons. It is wise to work on prevention—we dare not be innocent about the risk of nuclear violence in the world today.

SMARTER ABOUT RELIGION, CULTURE, AND NATIONAL SECURITY

It is hard for people to see culture; culture is so much a part of who we are that it is like a fish trying to notice water. It surrounds us and permeates society. Culture is primarily the way meaning is imposed on the world. Culture is the way people orient themselves in a meaningful way in the world. When you want to deeply understand culture, you are inevitably going to include religion as a major part of how meaning is made.[10] Religion is first, last, and always the way people tell themselves "what it means."

Thus, religion is an incredibly important part of what foreign policy experts call soft power. A "religion-in-culture" analysis is not even an "add-on" to the concept of soft power as much as it is a kind of "digging down" into the soft power premise. Now the challenge is to get analysts to actually see that religion is a deeply embedded part of culture. In other words, when we see religion as part of culture, we get smarter about smart power. In the last decade, Americans lost soft power around the world because our values (freedom and democracy) were contradicted by our actions (preemptive war and torture). We are only starting to get it back through some smarter connections between our values and our actions, but we have a long way to go.

Communicating respect for Islam as a religion, for example, is a prime way President Obama has applied religious language to this problem of the loss of soft power. Coupled with actions, such as closing Guantanamo, this is helping. It is also evidence that this new administration recognizes a broad soft power role for religion and values around the world. As the President said in his speech in Cairo, "I've come here to Cairo to seek a new beginning between the United States and Muslims around the world, one based on mutual interest and mutual respect, and one based upon the truth that America and Islam are not exclusive and need not be in competition. Instead, they overlap, and share common principles—principles of justice and progress; tolerance and the dignity of all human beings."[11]

We need to be ever more cognizant of the larger forces at play in the world, beyond categories of East and West, or Islamic and Christian, in order to understand why religion is such a powerful force, in both hard and soft power senses, in this time.

The reason religion is on the rise around the world is that people are disoriented by modern life—it's too much, it's too fast, and it's contradictory. The whole world lives in the digital age. After the election protests in Iran, no one can doubt that not only the United States but everywhere, people are wired, connected, and at the same time, experiencing the huge disconnections that the digital age imposes and even magnifies.

The sheer volume of modernity is destabilizing on both a personal and social level. It's not only American teenagers getting dumped in three or four different electronic applications. It's the way the Internet brings everything, every day in such a huge and unfiltered volume into billions of homes and offices. It's too much. So religion becomes a way to re-impose meaning on a world that seems ever more meaningless, chaotic, and even threatening.

We will not get wiser about national security without recognizing that the digital age is the human fall from innocence delivered at terabyte speed. But human beings constantly dream of Eden and so they are attracted to religions that offer a simple and fixed promise of the return to innocence. The greatest security threat we face in the world is from the rise of conservative religions that promise an escape to Eden or heaven or a version of paradise. And these religions are on the rise.[12] This is as true of conservative Christian dreams of a "Rapture" whisking them away to heaven as it is of the dreams fed to Islamic suicide bombers that though they die killing, they will wake up in paradise.

People do not only dream of innocence when it comes to national security, however. The dream of innocence is very compelling when it is the security of your pocketbook that is at stake. That's why Americans are tempted to believe that there is an "invisible hand" guiding the markets, the hand of God. And so nothing really bad can happen to our economy—or, if something bad happens to you like losing your job or your savings in a big market downturn, it's *your fault*, not the fault of the market.

EIGHT

GOD DOESN'T RUN MARKETS, PEOPLE DO

For many Americans today, trusting in the capitalist system is almost a form of religious belief. This has not always been the case, however. During the crash of the 1930s, Americans became deeply suspicious of financial institutions and of capitalism itself. Bankers were the bad guys in films during that time. They were portrayed as fat, self-satisfied, smoking big cigars, and destroying the "little guy" or "the forgotten man." In the brilliant 1933 film, _Dinner at Eight_, an honest businessman could not earn a living and the bankers were in cahoots with the corrupt business lobbies. Later, in the 1950s, came "Godless communism" and the perceived national security threat from the Soviet Union, and capitalism stood against communism in the name of God and nation. Americans came to believe that God is behind the market, guiding it with an "invisible hand." This became a sort of religious faith all by itself.

As was noted earlier, comedian Stephen Colbert calls faith in capitalism "moneytheism." "Moneytheism" is "the American faith in the free market." Colbert posits that Americans give the Lord's Prayer a slight twist, praying "give us this day our daily Mighty Dollar."[1] Sometimes it takes a comic to expose the unrealistic and yet powerful religious and cultural trends that underlie the almost mystical American faith in the "self-regulating" market. Amazingly enough, Karl Rove was still hoping for a "miracle" to be delivered

? Street vs Main Street

by the market in 2007 even as banks and mortgage institutions were failing and taking the world economy down with them. Now that's really trying to run the country on a wing and a prayer. "What really matters," said Rove, "is the miracle of the market…"[2]

These popular views were given academic credibility at the highest levels. An extreme faith in the self-regulating capacity of the market is sometimes also called "market fundamentalism." This is the ultracapitalist view most associated with the famous economist Milton Friedman. "Market fundamentalism" is the nearly unshakeable faith held by its true believers that the best economic results are obtained when the market is allowed to function without the restraints of regulation. This belief system launched the Reagan Revolution in the United States and the Thatcher Revolution in England. By the end of the 1970s, Friedman was one of the most admired economists in the world. Not so much now, however.

Conservative economists like to clothe the concept of unregulated capitalism in the idea of rationalism; they claim that the market is the best and most realistic regulator of the market itself because the market moves on solid financial information and then this information is used by objective, rational investors to determine value. Billionaire investor Warren Buffet skewered this view nicely when he observed, "I'd be a bum on the street with a tin cup if markets were always efficient."[3] What Buffet meant was that he got rich because he'd buy stocks that were undervalued and then make money when they went up. If stocks were always valued rationally, Buffet was saying, he would be poor. Anybody who watches the stock market should get that Buffet is right and Friedman is wrong; the market is not coldly rational; it is as much a cultural product as any other consumer item. There's a good reason Buffet is sometimes called the "Wizard of Omaha."

Indeed, I have compared Warren Buffet to the chief Wizard in the Harry Potter series, Albus Dumbledore. Buffet's wizardly wisdom, like that of Dumbledore, is "that there is no magic that can solve all your problems."[4] And that includes the "miracle" or the "magic" of the markets. The market is run by human beings and so it reflects human nature. And the market certainly reflects religious views of human nature and society as they are presented in our culture.

In a section of his book *Bad Money,* political and economic commentator Kevin Phillips explains exactly how conservative religion and market fundamentalism mutually reinforce one another, to the great detriment of the country and the world. He calls Christian fundamentalism the "enabler" of market fundamentalism and shows how conservative Christianity provided the cultural shift necessary so that ordinary Americans would become anesthetized to their previous suspicion of unregulated capitalism born in the 1930s.

Phillips observes that the complete breakdown in realistic thinking about how markets and financial systems actually do work has three sources: "homage to financial assets, market efficiency," and "evangelical, fundamentalist, and Pentecostal Christianity, infused with a millennial preoccupation with terrorism, evil, and Islam." These three legs of the stool caused the "de facto anesthetizing, over the last twenty years, of onetime populist southern and western" regions.[5]

Phillips understands the cultural significance and power of religion, a point he made very well in his earlier book, *American Theocracy.*[6] The point is that if a significant segment of the American population is preoccupied with expecting the Rapture at any moment, they really won't care that much about budget deficits or what's happening to the dollar. Evangelical centrists also understand how damaging the "Rapture" views are because they distract people from thinking realistically about how to improve this world now and keep them focused on the end of this world. Tim Weber, professor of Church History at Northern Baptist Theological Seminary says, "If Jesus may come at any minute, then long-term social reform or renewal are beside the point. It has a bad effect there."[7]

But conservatives had help in constructing our current economy. They had help from liberals.

LIBERALS AND MARKETS

Do liberals really provide an alternative to the conservative love of the unregulated market? First let me clarify what I mean by liberal. When I use the term liberal, I do not mean what the Ann Coulters or Rush Limbaughs of the world mean when they foam at the mouth about the how liberals are really closet Communists and out to destroy religion.

 Liberalism in the United States (liberalism means many other things around the world) is based on the idea of freedom of the individual. Liberalism is really at the foundation of the U.S. Constitution, especially in its protections of freedom of religion, of speech, and of the right for citizens to be treated equally. Freedom and equality are the enlightenment values that liberalism carries along in the United States. In religion, liberalism means that God can be experienced directly—you don't need a priest or even a church for that. People are free not just politically, but also spiritually.

In the New Deal in the 1930s, liberalism also came to be associated with the idea that the federal government can and should act when the economy is in trouble. In fact, it was during the

Depression, when the government pumped money into the economy, that the whole association of liberalism and government programs took hold. Liberals added "freedom from want" (in the immortal words of Franklin Roosevelt) to the list of freedoms they supported.

Franklin Roosevelt was a Democrat and the association of liberalism and the Democratic Party was cemented in his presidency. Beginning in the 1930s, Democrats became the political party of economic opportunity for working classes, immigrants, and the labor movement in general. Democrats were also the party of social opportunity in securing civil rights.

But that was then and this is now. In the last twenty-five years liberals have been portrayed as "left-wing" for their positions on social issues such as a woman's right to choose, or gay marriage. During the 1990s and Democrat Bill Clinton's presidency, when it came to the economy, there was little difference between the Clinton administration's approach to the markets and banking and the conservative Republican administration's both before and after him. Larry Summers, hired back in the Obama Administration, was Clinton's Secretary of the Treasury for the last year and half of the Clinton presidency. Summers was a big supporter of the Gramm-Leach-Billey Act of 1999 that lifted the banking regulations that FDR had put in place to protect Americans from another financial meltdown like the one that kicked off the Great Depression.

Why would the liberal Bill Clinton and his chief financial advisor support this?

Is it that they held too optimistic a view of human nature, especially when it came to the economy? Well, if so, it seems like their optimism about human nature extended as far as Wall Street.

In 1998, in testimony before the Senate, Summers said that we didn't need regulation for the new "credit-default swaps" because we could *trust* Wall Street. "The parties to these kinds of contracts are largely sophisticated financial institutions that would appear to be eminently capable of protecting themselves from fraud and counterparty insolvencies and most of which are already subject to basic safety and soundness regulation under existing banking and securities laws."[8]

Summers said this because he backed the Commodity Futures Modernization Act, which allowed these financial derivatives to be traded without any oversight or regulation. These are the "credit-default swaps" that most people both in and outside of the financial industry think were what really triggered the recent economic collapse.

The 'trusting Wall Street' concept was a big shift that happened in the swinging, more socially liberal 1990s. In the 1990s business became democratic; everybody invested. If you had $500 in a 401(k) plan, you were one of the great masses of folks who were now rooting for the stock market to keep going up, up, up. Investing was the new populism. "In decades previous, business had rewarded the well born and pompous, but now everything was different. In the nineties business was a *truth*-device; a friend of humanity; a powerful warrior for global democracy; a righteous enemy of pretense and falsehood."[9] Or so it sold itself to the average American through massive advertising and sloganeering.

An MCI commercial said it all. In 1996, MCI ran an add that invited its viewers to believe that we had effectively returned to the Garden of Eden, cleansed and purified of all racial, gender, and handicapping divisions, and with phone service! Images flashed up on the television, punctuated with an alternative-rock soundtrack, first of a little girl crossing out the word "race" and the voiceover intoning, "there is no race"; two women sitting in front of a computer, "there are no genders"; and a teenage girl doing sign language "there are no disabilities." And the company's slogan summed it all up, "Is this a great time or what?"[10]

In that same decade of the 1990s, however, workers mostly had a different view, because their seat at the table was being pushed back further and further. It was in the late 1980s and into the '90s when the salaries of ordinary workers and the CEO's of their companies started to separate. Workers' wages were flat or gained very little; and management salaries went through the roof. Huge bonuses being paid to corporate CEOs, regardless of how the actual company performed, wasn't a new thing in the twenty-first century. It had been going on for almost twenty years. Union membership went down and down, and unions themselves were under systematic attack by 'consultants' hired by business leaders to prevent unionization in their companies.

But who spoke for these workers? In the business-is-democratic 1990s, the party of labor had become the other pro-business party. As Thomas Frank points out in *What's the Matter With Kansas?*, one thing that pushed Kansas to the frontlines of the culture wars was that the real suffering of people who live in Kansas, their economic suffering, wasn't being addressed by anybody. The people in Kansas were angry because their towns were crumbling, their businesses closing and whole sections of the state were in environmental decline. But this populist anger was successfully directed not at business but at Darwinian evolutionary theory and homosexuality and abortion.

That happened because there was no real political alternative. "By all rights the people in Wichita, Shawnee and Garden City should today be flocking to the party of Roosevelt, not deserting it. Culturally speaking however, that option is simply not available to them anymore. Democrats no longer speak to the people on the losing end of a free-market system that is becoming more brutal and more arrogant by the day."[11]

But we can't totally blame liberalism here. It is true that Clinton and the "new" Democrats crafted a pro-business strategy. And it is true that Bill Clinton was a pretty classic big government, social liberal. But liberalism has historically not been a grassroots movement of working class people, as Frank suggests. That history belongs more to progressivism and populism. What is really needed is a grassroots movement to bring Kansas back to its senses about why the people there have such a poor economy and poor education system.

Liberal individualism and confidence in human nature and human institutions are not the stuff of which grassroots movements are made. People at the bottom, people like my grandparents who immigrated from Hungary as teenagers and who worked their whole lives in the sweatshops of the New York garment district, joined labor movements. They did that not because they thought they should "trust" management, or because they trusted government to help them out, but because they didn't trust them. They had first-hand experience of management and the labor laws of New York City and they knew that both management and government couldn't be trusted around a glass corner.

The history of the labor movement and social reform is more closely associated with what is called progressivism and, in religious terms, "the Social Gospel." Both Republican and Democratic reformers have at times allied themselves with the progressive movement. Progressivism is less individualistic than liberalism and also less idealistic. Progressives have tended to be reformers on the excesses of the wealthy elites and the real effects of grinding poverty on people and their communities.

What we need today to really fix what's broken in our economy is a real populist movement.

THE OLD POPULISM

I know you might find this hard to believe today, especially after what happened in Kansas, but at one time it was the biblical conservatives who defended the working class against the worst excesses of capitalism. William Jennings Bryan, the great orator and politician, became famous, as was noted earlier, for his role in opposing the teaching of evolution. Bryan, however, was also one of the most prominent defenders of working class people in the late nineteenth and early twentieth centuries. He was an advocate for peace, a critic of banks and railroads, and as a devout Presbyterian, *as well,* a big opponent of Darwinian evolutionary theory.

What religious conservatives and liberals today do not remember, as was also pointed out earlier, is that Bryan's opposition to Darwin was that he thought that evolution's theory of "survival of the fittest" was being used as an excuse for the worst excesses of capitalism against poor and working class people. It wasn't just the biblical creation story that Bryan was defending, he was defending the common folk against the terrible conditions of industrialization and their scientific justification. He was known as a defender of populism—that is, as a defender of the ordinary people against the elites. His nickname was "The Great Commoner."

Instead, what is remembered about Bryan at all comes from the Broadway stage and Hollywood. Bryan became the voice of irrational doctrine against reason and modern science and *freedom.* The so-called "Scopes Monkey Trial" was dramatized both on stage in 1955 in *Inherit the Wind,* and in a more famous film in

1960. In the movie, the pompous William Jennings Bryan character, played by Fredric March, stutters through his defense of the literal biblical creation story. The great lawyer Clarence Darrow character, meanwhile, is the relentless voice of reason and the modern age. Both the play and the movie were actually more of a warning against McCarthyism than any kind of actual retelling of the 1925 Scopes trial.

The real William Jennings Bryan spoke for a kind of economic populism that no longer exists in either religious conservatism or in religious liberalism. This is a tragedy, because it is becoming more and more apparent that Americans need to find the moral roots of the struggle for the dignity of ordinary workers.

The reason this is important is that "survival of the fittest" as a way of describing capitalism is back. Larry Summers sold the idea of applying "survival of the fittest" Darwinian interpretations to business. At the Kennedy School of Government in 2000, Summers said, "The traditional industrial economy was a Newtonian system of opposing forces, checks and balances... While, in contrast, *the right metaphors for the new economy are Darwinian, with the fittest surviving.*"[12]

THE NEW POPULISM: THE DIGNITY OF WORK

A job is not just a job. It is the way human beings work together and the material conditions of reality to create a world for themselves and their posterity. Cain the metalworker founds a city and names it after his son, Enoch. I'm like Cain in this, my job, whether it is the work I do caring for my children or when I teach a class, is absolutely fundamental to my human nature and its expression, and I do it for my family as well as for myself.

This connection between work and human dignity is at the core of a moral vision to guide and shape a new populism. This populism has its roots in the "social gospel" at the beginning of the twentieth century, a Christian interpretation of what a good economy should look like and the principles on which it should be based. People need both a means to practical economic advancement and respect for their human dignity and equal worth.

Economic well-being is a way to achieve practical goodness in an economy. This moral vision is not idealistic, but realistic, and it is not incompatible with market economies. Market economies allow for human creativity and initiative in a way that centralized economies often do not.

Pope John Paul II brought a unique experience to his work in the papacy because he had grown up in Poland under Communist rule and he supported the labor movement in its protests against the exploitation of workers in that system. He brought that experience to his reflections on human nature and the economy. He concluded that decent working conditions are central to human dignity. In his well-known encyclical, *On Human Work*, he states that work is fundamental to the truth of the human condition. Through work, people become who they are intended to be. Through work, human beings share "in the activity of the Creator" (Laborem Exercens, V.25).

Human dignity is not passive, but active. It is something that we *practice*. Human potential is fulfilled when people have the means to express their creativity and an important way they do that is through work. By the same token, when people are denied the ability to fulfill their human potential through work, this is a denial of the dignity of what it means to be human. Society thus has both a practical and a moral obligation to promote economic systems that allow for the widest possible expression of human potential through work.[13]

Few religious people today, either on the Right or on the Left, really seem to recognize the fundamental link between sound economic practices and respect for human dignity. We must reclaim the moral vision of economic progress through a deep-seated commitment to helping create and sustain economic systems that draw upon and stimulate human creativity.

In the last decade, however, our economic system has produced fewer and fewer jobs, and the jobs it has produced are in the lower-paying, service sectors. Tax cuts for the wealthy, wage suppression tactics, undercutting unions, and other deliberate practices created a decade of declining or stagnant wages and slow or no real job growth. These tactics increase profits at the expense of workers. Often Americans have had to work two or even three jobs to make ends meet, sacrificing family time and even adequate rest to make a modest living. These kinds of jobs do not honor human dignity; they erode a sense of self-worth and contribute to a sense of helplessness and despair. They are a direct attack on the fundamental dignity and worth of human beings as expressed through their work.

So even though the economy has been "productive," from the perspective of morality it has been a failure. There are economists, however, who are also saying that not only have these economic policies been a moral failure; they have been a practical failure as well. As the Center for American Progress' Michael Ettlinger argues, "economic policies with tax cuts for corporations and the wealthy as their centerpiece have simply failed to produce strong economic growth by a variety of measures." The growth has been illusory; and real sustaining change to strengthen our economy has been shortchanged.

Economic policies of tax cuts for corporations and the wealthy are the result of political processes that favor those economic interests over the majority of the people. In 1932, Reinhold Niebuhr wrote from the depths of another economic downturn that, "economic power has become irresponsible in society." Niebuhr believed that economic interests had simply overwhelmed the political process through an excess of power.[14]

PEOPLE AND THE MARKETS THEY MAKE

Markets are tools of economic exchange. God doesn't run them, and the people who actually do run them aren't saints. That's okay. We really don't live in the Garden of Eden where everyone acts with the purest possible motives and never, ever sins. Larry Summers might think you just can shut your eyes and 'trust' Wall Street, but anybody who has read Genesis would think twice before doing that. People are more like Cain than they are like Jesus.

Knowing what markets are really like and how they really operate can help us run them better so that they will do what they do best, create good-paying jobs for ordinary Americans, and be restrained from exploitive business practices, whether of individuals or the environment. Theories of markets actually assume that people will act according to their self-interest and not from a disinterested love of others. This may not be inspiring, but it is pretty realistic. This has been known for a very long time. In 1776, Adam Smith, sometimes considered the "father" of modern economics, related human nature and how markets work, "It is not from the benevolence of the butcher, the brewer, or the bakers that we expect our dinner, but from their regard to their own interest. We address ourselves not to their humanity but to their self-love, and never talk to them of our own necessities but of their advantage."[15]

MARKETS AFTER THE FALL

We can understand the term "fall" here in two senses: the fall of the stock market because of the financial crisis of 2008–2009, and the fall as the human capacity to be both creative and destructive, foolish and wise, greedy and generous, in short, to be human.

After we as taxpayers have poured trillions of dollars into financial institutions, have we learned anything? One thing I have learned, and this is more from reading the story "A" in Genesis than anything else, is that we have to put the realities of human nature back into our financial systems. Somehow we need to uncouple the runaway freight train that linked excessive risk to excessive reward *with taxpayers bearing the burden of failure.* That's not capitalism and its risk/reward equation. That kind of threesome of risk/reward/taxpayer subsidy will spell the death of capitalism. Our economy will then be captive to these ever larger boom and bust cycles. And the American people will suffer even more from each downturn because this slow recovery looks to be another 'jobless recovery' like the last two recoveries from recession.

Regulate! Cap executive salaries! Break them up and make them small enough to fail! These are some of the preventive measures that are being proposed. If we take human nature into account from the time of the expulsion from the Garden of Eden, we ignore human nature in the digital age at our peril in making changes.

While we may be in agreement that too big to fail is a problem, how big is too big? Too big is certainly the kind of monopoly that drives out competition; that must be prevented with regulation. Monopolies that undermine competition actually destroy one of the things that do work in capitalism, as competition is a driver of economic productivity in a capitalist system. Yet, big is good in the digital age because big helps firms get economies of scale and scope that they need in a global economic climate.

So why not regulate them up to their eyebrows? That should solve the problem. Or will it? Some things can be done certainly. If it walks like a bank and it talks like a bank and it works like a bank, regulate it like a bank no matter what it calls itself. But beyond that, there's not much regulation that can really help. Regulators are always regulating the problems of the past, and the human beings who are attracted to high finance are creative people. They are already finding ways to get around the new regulations that are not even yet in place. That's why firms like Goldman Sachs are making money like mad again, because they're already taking on risk again.

Regulators are also human and therefore fallible; and they are paid less than those they oversee—and they operate at the behest of politicians who are being lobbied by the finance industry on both sides of the aisle. This is a system that is loaded with human frailty and human creativity. It is a system that is certainly not run by God, but it's not run by the devil either. It is a complicated and increasingly interlocked system that is not driven by transcendent values of generosity and kindness. It is a system that may have many in it who mean well, but they mean well in a narrow and personal sense at best. If they have a sense of responsibility, it is not for the well-being of society at large, but for shareholders or voters, depending on their place in the system. And voters, like myself, don't understand regulation and I know I certainly don't vote for my congressional representative, or our Senators, based on their views on the regulation of the financial industry.

Capitalism works as a productive economic system when the risk takers have their own skin in the game, so to speak. Where can we actually change this system so that self-interest will once again, like Adam Smith thought, be working for us rather than against us? Only this time, make self-interest the engine that works to prevent boom and bust cycles that don't also stifle economic productivity and job creation. We need to understand what we might call "Cain-sian" economics, that is, the regulatory role self-interest can play in capitalism. But we dare not be naïve that self-interest will just naturally take over—Alan Greenspan thought this and it was plainly wrong in practice.

An example of "Cain-sian" economics is making regulation follow the money. Make money, i.e., capital, the centerpiece of the new regulatory structure because that will follow our religious insight into human nature. First, link managers' bonuses to a bank's bonds. Now, managers get bonuses even if a bank has catastrophic losses. That must change. The self-interest must be redirected toward internal risk management and personal reward. There would be far fewer economically dangerous practices if the people making those decisions knew that their own income was directly tied to their risk assessments. That's about the most important change we could make.

Also, require that banks have more capital. Higher capital requirements would bring the skin of the shareholders into the game as well. If it's their money at stake, shareholders become part of the regulatory function because they will not stand for practices that put their money at risk. Shareholders won't do this because they are angels, but because they are self-interested and our regulation has put their self-interest back into the equation. These means banks would have to have more capital reserves, but it also means that the U.S. taxpayer is no longer the de facto capital reserve for these financial institutions.

The theological interpretation of human nature is my contribution to the recommendations above; the idea to link risk to the performance of managers and the profits of shareholders is the suggestion of an editorial in *The Economist*. This editorial concludes: "Regulation [of this kind] cannot prevent financial crises altogether, but it can minimize the devastation. Loading banks with equity slows the creation of credit, but the reward for a healthy financial system is faster growth over the long term. There are three trillion reasons to think that trade-off is worth it."[16]

It is rare for economists and theologians to share ideas, but in this wired world, with the capacity for a world-wide banking system to bring down not just one country, but much of the world's economies, we have to try everything we can to get wiser about human beings and how they really behave in the economies they make. I hope "public theologians" will step up to this challenge, and that economists will listen to us, and we will listen to them.

MARKETS ARE NOT INNOCENT, AND NEITHER ARE THE PEOPLE WHO RUN THEM

It's not capitalism that's broken per se; it's the understanding of human nature that is used to guide capitalism that is broken. You cannot take self-interest out of the equation without letting in a horde of risk takers who are rewarded whether the system goes boom or bust. That's just asking for trouble, and trouble is what we've got.

So, put the risk back and make the people who take the risk, bear the risk. The world is wired, and the risks and rewards are increasing right along with the digital revolution. As Steve Jobs and the Apple logo tell us, the age of the Internet has increased our desire for good and for ill. So it is especially critical in a wired world that we base our financial regulations on human nature as it really is, not as we wish it to be. Financial innocence is what will really "bring down the house."

First, we have to recognize that if something sounds too good to be ture, it almost always is. In the complications of human life lived after the "fall," if something is too sensible, *it may also be too good* to come true. The one flaw in the sensible economic and theological approach outlined above, in fact, is that it won't happen unless legislators make it happen. That's where our system is truly broken. The power of the financial lobby and its influence on lawmakers is such that trying to put a tight risk/reward structure back into our financial system will be met with tremendously powerful resistance by those financial interests who want to keep the U.S. taxpayer as their reserve capital fund. And if ever there were a group that represented the capacity of human beings to act out of self-interest, it is the lobbying industry. K Street is not an innocent place to work.

The best thing we could have Congress do is understand that the stories in Genesis are not about literal creation, but about what people are actually like. The story of Adam and Eve, and their children, Cain and Abel, provides the essential insights into how we can negotiate our individual relationships and our public policy in a way that is smarter, because it is far less innocent about human nature.

There is some good news ahead, because the twenty-something generation, sometimes called the Millennals, appears to be far less naïve about human nature. They plan to save the planet from the worst effects of climate change too.

NINE

THE MILLENNIALS: GREEN
WITHOUT THE GARDEN?

College freshmen at Emory University made a music video to launch their group "MillennialBeacon" in January of 2009 and posted it on YouTube. In their video, Coldplay's haunting hit "Lost" accompanies images evoking genocide in Sudan, a picture of the earth's curve as the sun comes over the edge, smoke coming out of a hole in one of the World Trade Center Towers on 9/11, the mushroom cloud from an atomic bomb, the London bus bombing, a street sign named "Recession," a Palestinian child holding a sign "Terror is our common enemy," windmills, solar panels, and people demonstrating in the streets.[1] The song "Lost" by Coldplay, the breakout British music group of the new millennium, is a perfect choice for these young people to have used in their challenging video; they are members of the Millennial Generation, those who have come into adulthood in the new millennium. They are wired, they think in images, and they are not naïve about the problems faced by their generation.

Coldplay's lyrics underline the Millennials' sober assessment of their age and their situation: "Just because I'm losing, Doesn't mean I'm lost, Doesn't mean I'll stop…Just because I'm hurting, Doesn't mean I'm hurt, Doesn't mean I didn't get what I deserved, No better and no worse." No better and no worse. No illusions about the problems, and hence no illusions about being able to solve them easily. The students claim in their video, "We are 75 million strong." That's a generation of significant size, and increasing influence.

This generation that Tweets and tries to change the world using Facebook and YouTube does not dream of Eden, at least many of them do not. They're often very realistic. With two wars, accelerating climate change, and the largest economic downturn since the Great Depression, they have a lot on their plates. They are also not finding a lot of connection in their wired lives.

The term "Millennials" refers to young people aged 13–29 who mostly did not want to be called "Generation Y," i.e., the demographic that followed the alienated and absent "Generation X."[2] They are millennial because in general they reached adulthood in the new millennium. The Millennials are really the first wired generation. They have grown up using computers, and the new media of the Internet such as email, texting, instant messaging, YouTube, Facebook, and Twitter. This has led them to also be called the "Net Generation" or "First Digitals," both labels that have not stuck. Pepsi-Cola tried to brand this generation as "Generation Next" in an advertising campaign that was abandoned in 1998. Like Douglas Coupland refusing the offer from Gap to become an advertising spokesman for Generation X, the Millennials are more than a little suspicious of obvious ploys to manipulate them with advertising. Many of them are far more sophisticated about the uses of media than those who are trying to pitch them soft drinks.

The Millennials are considered the first "green" generation; they are highly educated about environmental issues and three-quarters of them say that they feel it's "important or very important" to get involved in the green movement. They live green.

Eighty-seven percent say they recycle; 84 percent turn off lights when not in use; 80 percent reduce water use; 73 percent use energy-efficient light bulbs. They participate in Earth Day; especially the 18–21 year-olds, and more than half of them want to learn more about the environment.[3]

In the 1970s and 1980s, the typical environmentalist was white, female, and well-educated. This is no longer exclusively the case. African American, Asian, and Hispanic Millennials, especially English-speaking Hispanics, also show an increased concern for the environment, though this is still far less than among whites.[4]

The Millennials (along with the iGeneration, those born after the mid-1990s), combine their web-savvy with their commitment to the environment. Seventy-nine percent of Millennials say they use the Internet as their main source of information about the environment.[5] They are both wired and green; they are also anxious and feel disconnected from larger social institutions, especially organized religion. In a 2010 Pew Forum on Religion and Public Life study, "Millennials and Religion," researchers found, "Compared with their elders today, young people are much less likely to affiliate with any religious tradition or to identify themselves as part of a Christian denomination."[6] In addition, they found that, "In their social and political views, young adults are clearly more accepting than older Americans of homosexuality, more inclined to see evolution as the best explanation of human life, and less prone to see Hollywood as threatening their moral values."[7] What the Pew study does not address, but what is key to the argument of this book, is that young adults not only do not see Hollywood as threatening their values, they are getting their theological views of the world *from* Hollywood. Because they are not part of religious institutions, and learning from them, they have to use whatever other sources they can find, and Hollywood is a formative choice for them.

DREAMING OF . . . THE MATRIX

As the first wave of the Millennial Generation reached 15–18 years of age, many of them saw *The Matrix*. *The Matrix* is a 1999 film starring Keanu Reeves. This blockbuster gave rise to two other Matrix films, *The Matrix Reloaded* and *The Matrix Revolution*. The original film is widely regarded as the best in the series.

The Matrix is *the* Garden of Eden narrative for the first completely wired generation.[8] This hugely successful and influential film both captured and influenced the wired generation. It also gave powerful expression to its deep anxiety both about computer technology and about the degradation of the environment in the increasingly technology-driven world the Millennials love and hate, crave and fear. The Millennial Generation does not dream of Eden. *The Matrix* took them to a computer-generated Eden and it was a nightmare.

For those who are not part of the Millennial Generation, the plot of *The Matrix* revolves around a computer programmer, Thomas A. Anderson, who leads a secret life as a hacker. His online name is "Neo." When the peculiar question "What is the Matrix?" keeps appearing on his screen, Neo wants to learn more—his curiosity leads him to a strange character called "Morpheus." Morpheus asks Neo if he wants to really learn the truth about the Matrix. Neo says he does and Morpheus gives him a red pill. Like Alice in Wonderland, he swallows the red pill. But unlike Alice, Neo falls into reality, not out of it.

Neo finds himself naked, floating in a liquid-filled pod and connected by wires to a huge mechanical tower. Other naked humans are also floating in pods and connected as well. Morpheus rescues him from this horror.

Neo learns from Morpheus, who unplugs him from computer-generated reality, that the year is really 2199, not 1999, and his body was being used as an energy source by machines that have taken over the world. The machines pacify the humans in their pods by connecting them to a computer-generated and completely non-existent reality.

In the early twenty-first century, Morpheus explains, humans and machines fought for control of earth. The humans tried to destroy the machines by creating huge black clouds to cut off their access to solar power. This scorched-earth defense wrecked the environment, but it did not succeed in defeating the machines. The machines started to use humans as their power source and thus created the Matrix.

Morpheus and some other escaped humans are still carrying on the war against the machines and the machines are tracking them and attempting to destroy them.

There is a socket in the back of Neo's head that was used to connect him and the other humans to the Matrix dream. Morpheus uses it to connect Neo to his computer and thus Neo is able to download huge amounts of knowledge directly into his brain. He becomes a formidable opponent of the intelligent machines that created and run the Matrix.

The climax of the film is when Neo learns to manipulate the computer-generated reality of the Matrix—he can dodge the bullets the agents of the Matrix shoot at him. Eventually Neo is able to perceive the Matrix as the streaming lines of green code it really is. He is no longer dreaming and he realizes he is incredibly powerful in the computer-generated alternate reality because he is awake and aware.

The earpieces of the wired generation's blue-tooth technology may not be implanted in their heads, at least not yet. But this generation has grown up connected to technology in an incredibly intimate way. It is the way Millennials acquire information, pursue relationships, often do their school work or jobs, and now do their politics. It is their source of entertainment. The Internet is part of war in many ways including cyberattacks on human rights activists and their online communication tools. Protestors use the Internet to fight back. Twitter helped young Iranians protest an unjust election.

Millennials are not innocently dreaming that technology will save them and the planet. They know technology too well and it is a source of anxiety. The innocent dreams of the computer-generated Matrix were a complete lie—the real truth may be that the Internet is controlling humanity instead of the other way around. Millennials know technology *is* already controlling us. This knowledge makes them realize how dangerous it is for humans to be tempted to dream of Eden. "Agent Smith" explains that the first Matrix didn't work because the machines tried to make a perfect world, an Eden, and the human beings connected to that program rebelled against it. The human beings wanted their "fall" from innocence.

> *Agent Smith*: Did you know that the first Matrix was designed to be a perfect human world? Where no one suffered, where everyone would be happy. It was a disaster. No one would accept the program. Entire crops [humans in their pods] were lost. Some believed we lacked the programming language to describe your perfect world. But I believe that, as a species,

human beings define their reality through suffering and misery. The perfect world was a dream that your primitive cerebrum kept trying to wake up from.

For the Millennials, war with machines, with technology, is not out in the open like Jules Verne's *War of the Worlds*. The war with machines for the Internet generation is in your head and in your imagination. You are freed by technology and you fear you are its slave. You learn about how to save the environment from machines, but could it be that the machines will ultimately be the cause of the complete destruction of the environment? In *The Matrix* "Agent Smith," who is trying to kill Neo, describes humans as the real cause of the environmental destruction of the planet. Agent Smith sounds a lot like a card-carrying member of Earth First! "Human beings are a disease, a cancer of this planet. You're a plague and we [the computer generated enforcers] are the cure."

Millennials do not dream nuclear nightmares; their nightmares come from another source. Millennials wonder why, when they have so much technological power at their fingertips, do they feel so powerless and so anxious at the same time? Millennials do not dream of Eden—they live a waking dream where they can instantly connect to almost anybody, anywhere. And they fear they are more and more alone because of it. The economic decline since the fall of 2008 has only aggravated this anxiety. Thus, this exchange between Morpheus and Neo:

> *Morpheus*: The Matrix is everywhere. It is all around us. Even now, in this very room. You can see it when you look out your window or when you turn on your television. You can feel it when you go to work…when you go to church…when you

pay your taxes. It is the world that has been pulled over your
eyes to blind you from the truth.

Neo: What truth?

Morpheus: That you are a slave, Neo. Like everyone else you
were born into bondage. Into a prison that you cannot taste
or see or touch. A prison for your mind.

Millennials are freed by being the first completely wired generation, and yet, at a deep level, they also fear that technology
enslaves them. Theirs is, in every sense, a love/hate relationship
with technology.

ZOMBIES AHEAD

The first decade of the New Millennium has had many sur-
prises, some of them, like the attacks of 9/11, very violent. In
Austin, Texas, in 2009, there was an attack of a different kind,
an attack by zombies. Electronic road signs that usually contain
messages of caution about road conditions changed. Instead
of the usual safety messages, the signs read "Caution! Zombies
Ahead!" or "Zombies in Area! Run for Cold Climates" or "Nazi
Zombies."[9] Computer hackers had gone to considerable trouble
to override these password-protected programs that run the
messages on these kinds of road signs. Highway authorities were
not amused.

What is it with all the zombies recently? I came out of a hotel
in Boston around the same time period and ran into a crowd of
hundreds of zombies walking peacefully toward the harbor—no
murderous attacks or brain-eating were reported. These were,
apparently, just living human beings who liked to dress like

zombies, not actual zombies. In many cities, Millennials in particular are dressing up like zombies and convening.

Zombies, to define them properly, are dead folks who climb out of their graves and eat the brains of the living. They were definitively portrayed this way in *Night of the Living Dead*. That zombies should suddenly break out now, at the end of the first decade of the New Millenium, takes some pondering. In my view, the zombie phenomenon is part rave and part a social/political anxiety response by the wired generation. If nothing else, the hacker skill needed to get around a password protected road sign demonstrates Millennial ability. In fact, when the North Koreans were suspected of cyber attacks on American and South Korean computers over the July 4, 2009 weekend, the attacks were orchestrated through "zombie computers," computers programmed to mindlessly send reams of data that overwhelm computer systems.[10]

Dressing up like a zombie and walking around may be fun, but it is also a peaceful, almost passive statement that reality is not what it appears to be, and that much of the world is mindless. Zombies could be all around, wreaking havoc with society, but everybody is pretending not to notice. That, at least, is the premise of *Pride and Prejudice and Zombies*, a book that appeared in the spring of 2009 and is a collaboration between the dead woman, Jane Austen, and a living (that is, non-zombie) author, Seth Grahame-Smith, himself a Millennial.

Smith places the rigid, mannered society that Austen described so wonderfully in her delicate prose, over an outbreak of zombism. Elizabeth Bennet, known to Austen fans as a singularly feisty heroine, is also now a trained warrior. She is one of the few people awake to the zombie menace, and she keeps a lethal dagger strapped to her leg.

She is not above contemplating slaughtering non-zombies as well. When she first meets the haughty Mr. Darcy at a ball, she contemplates following him out to the garden and slitting his throat for his dismissal of her person. But then zombies attack the ball, feasting on the hapless guests. One poor guest, Mrs. Long, cannot free herself "as two female dreadfuls bit into her head, cracking her skull like a walnut, and sending a shower of dark blood spouting as high as the chandeliers." Elizabeth is obliged to behead many zombies as she works her way around the room. These undead, brain-eating hordes are, in polite society, either ignored completely or referred to as "unmentionables." Mrs. Bennet believes that, "[A]part from the attack, the evening altogether passed off pleasantly for the whole family."[11]

Apart from being incredibly funny, *Pride and Prejudice and Zombies* is a symptom of the frustration of the Millennial Generation, at the economy, most of all, but also at how the reach of this generation, even in its political hopes with the Obama campaign, continually exceed its grasp.

Zombism is a uniquely wired generation form of protest/anxiety attack as it represents the disconnected nature of the most technologically connected generation of all. Zombism is, of course, only expressed by a few—but in the way that speaks volumes for all those who are wired and frustrated and without other resources to interpret their situation. When computers are programmed to send repeated emails to shut down an electronic site, like happened to Facebook and Twitter or even to various government agencies, it is called a zombie attack. Mindless repetition of computer generated email is a form of zombism. It is a clue to how alienating it can be, being the first digital generation.

Millennials tend to go it alone. They are very suspicious of institutions in general. They have been shunning religious institutions and community in increasing numbers for more than a decade. This gives them fewer historic resources to interpret their situation. From war, to the economy, to the experience they have that the more they are connected to others through technology, the more they are actually disconnected. Thus, Millennials are taking their meaning where they can find it.

Millennials think they have to make up their religious interpretation of the world and so they use a little of this and a little of that. That may leave them with zombies as a resource. And, well, there's also Zen.

MILLNENIALS: SPIRITUAL BUT NOT RELIGIOUS

Not only did *The Matrix* speak directly to the hopes and fears of the wired and green generation, it exactly captured their eclectic religious life as well. Millennials are deeply suspicious of institutions of all kinds, but especially religious institutions. They are also deeply suspicious of Eden and they do not dream of a perfect world. In fact, they have been promised that too many times from too many sources, religious, political, and technological. Millennials know the dream of a perfect world is a perfect nightmare.

The typical Millennial says that he or she does not belong to a religious institution. Millennials are leaving traditional religious institutions in droves.[12] They will say, "I'm spiritual but not religious." A 25-year-old's Facebook page declares his "religious affiliation" is "physically optimistic." Another Millennial replies to a survey on his attitudes and beliefs toward religion, "I see a difference too between being religious and being spiritual. Being spiritual is like what you believe yourself and church doesn't really matter."[13]

In 2009 the Pew Forum on Religion and Public Life published an extensive survey that documents the changing landscape of American religion. In the demographic section, the survey indicated the marked decline in formal religious affiliation of the 18–29 year-old age group, a point that was expanded in the larger, 2010 study. Across the board, from evangelical Protestant to Muslim, this largest generation since the Baby Boomers is moving away from institutional religion in droves.[14]

Churches and synagogues and even mosques do not seem relevant to this generation; religious institutions do not appear to address their lives. "I think that in a hundred years organized religion will be obsolete in this world. I think although we say, 'I am Christian, I am a Jew or Muslim, or whatever, I think most people find it for themselves. I don't think we can relate to the old books as well as people before did. We may have beliefs based on them but it is more personal. We believe in what we want to believe in."[15]

Historically black churches and Evangelical Hispanics are holding on to their young people at slightly higher rates (4 percent)— Catholics are losing young people (especially Hispanics) to Evangelicals or to "unaffiliated." African American and Hispanic males are both far more likely to reject organized religion than are their female peers. Yet, Millennials in general continue to reply to pollsters that they believe in God or a higher power.

So, what kind of spirituality is this spirituality that is not religious? Partly, the spiritual language is taken from Zen Buddhism. Zen is now part of American culture, both through the increasing practice of yoga by many Millennials, and by the use of some Buddhist themes in popular culture. Zen Buddhism is a huge part of the way in which *The Matrix* writers presented the problem of reality and mind in the film.

Zen Buddhism is centered in a meditative practice that emphasizes direct experience rather than formal creeds or scriptures. Wisdom passes from teacher to student, not in words but through the practice of meditation and eventually mind to mind.

The use of Zen in *The Matrix* is fairly simple and straightforward. The premise of *The Matrix* is that reality is computer generated, not what people think they see and feel. Buddhists believe that the world is an illusion and we have to break out of that illusion in order to find enlightenment. Neo goes through a kind of Buddhist journey of enlightenment as he struggles to see and then manipulate the Matrix. The following exchange between Neo and a boy is typically "pop Buddhist" in content. The boy has told Neo to bend a spoon with his mind and Neo has failed to do it.

> *Boy*: Do not try and bend the spoon. That's impossible. Instead...only try to realize the truth.
> *Neo*: What truth?
> *Boy*: There is no spoon.
> *Neo*: There is no spoon?
> *Boy*: Then you'll see, that it is not the spoon that bends, it is only yourself.

Buddhism emphasizes that achieving enlightenment is achieving the inherent Buddha-nature that all sentient beings have. In Buddhism there is no "fall" from the perfection of the Garden of Eden; there is only the journey to enlightenment and that journey is totally in your mind. This is why the practice of meditation is central to Zen Buddhism as it is through meditation practice that the person discovers his or her own inner Buddha-nature and thus achieves enlightenment.

Of course, actual Buddhist enlightenment takes years and years of intense work in meditation with knowledgeable teachers. What floats through American pop culture in films and even in most yoga classes is a kind of Xerox copy of Buddhism that is based on the old "I'm Okay, You're Okay" psychology of the 1960s. It is often a very thin shield against a culture that is perceived as uncertain and even threatening.

Neo does not overcome the threat of the Matrix by meditation and chanting. The Matrix is constantly identified as "the enemy" along with the machines like "Agent Smith." The level of violence in Millennial pop culture in general is enormous. Submachine gun fire, torture, and vicious hand-to-hand combat are a constant in *The Matrix* and subsequent films. Millennials may claim to be "spiritual but not religious," but theirs is a deeply conservative Christian view of the struggle between good and evil, not a peaceful Buddhist interpretation of the journey of mind toward enlightenment.

The Matrix is as violent as *The Passion of the Christ* and actually has a very similar theme. Neo is constantly asked if he is "the One" who has been prophesied. Neo, like the earthly Jesus, keeps denying he is "the One" until it becomes clear through his abilities to take on Satan (i.e., the evil Matrix) that he is, in fact, "the One" who will save humanity. Neo finally does save humanity through violence.

It is the astounding levels of violence in *The Matrix* that reveal its profoundly Christian roots. Its violence is the primal violence that is so much a part of the traditional Christian reading of the story of Cain and Abel. The Matrix as threat to human life isn't really an illusion that we can overcome through meditation. The Matrix is out to kill you, it's the enemy, and the good guys have to shoot first and ask questions later. This is the same kind of dualism of good and evil that underlies the conservative Christian theology of the Rapture novels, and American culture in general.[16] If John Wayne had been born a Millennial, would he have played the part of Neo? Or, put another way, isn't Neo a digital cowboy, saving the frontier town from the outlaws?

The fundamental problem for Millennials is that, in fact, their religious institutions have failed them. They are so right about that. Through inattention, scandal, and general spiritual fatigue, the more liberal to middle-of-the-road religious institutions have not understood and responded to the spiritual crisis in the lives of Millennials.

Conservative Christianity has tried to reach out to this generation with more energy and more programming, but conservatives too have failed to understand and interpret the digital age in a way that makes sense to the kind of connected/disconnected feelings Millennials often have. Also, conservative religion has not been able to connect with the environmental concerns of young people and they are also turned off by the blatant anti-homosexual messages of conservative religion. Their generation is markedly more accepting of gay, lesbian, bi-sexual and transgendered people. Millennials realize that being gay isn't a problem for their generation—rather, their problems are being able to breathe the air in twenty years, and not retire in poverty.

Millennial's problems are both spiritual and religious. The impact on them of being the first digital generation is huge and it has been totally ignored by conservatives, mainstream and liberals alike. Millennials are right that they are on their own; it is not that they have abandoned religious institutions; religious institutions have abandoned them. They are having to make their own way, find their own interpretations and use what they can to make sense of this wired world. They have to take their religious meaning where they can find it, and if that is yoga classes, movies, zombie raves, and some blogs, that's what they will use.

In the meantime, they are trying to help save their planet and their society.

LOVE YOUR NEIGHBOR AS YOURSELF... MILLENNIALS VOLUNTEER

No organization better illustrates the service commitments of the Millennials than Teach for America. Teach for America has a simple and easy to understand mission. It is a non-profit that recruits recent college graduates and professionals to teach for two years in low-income communities throughout the United States. Teach for America has two goals. The first is that its recruits make a positive, short-term impact on their students. The second is that its corps members become life-long advocates for improved public educational quality.

TFA was founded by Millennials, for Millennials. Its founder, Wendy Kopp, did her senior thesis at Princeton in 1989 on ways to help eliminate educational inequality in the United States. She began the organization in 1990 and more than 14,000 corps members have served successfully.[17] The growth of TFA has been exponential. From a beginning group of 500 recruits, in 2008, a record 35,000 applications were received for approximately 3,700 positions. It is a testimony to the service orientation of Millennials, as well as to their longing for really making a difference in the world.

THE ECONOMY: A "FALL" FOR
MILLENNIALS?

As the new "boom" generation, Millennials excite enormous interest—not only from public theologians like me, but from the sociologists and, of course, the marketing people. Marketing blogs are tracking questions like "how are twenty-somethings coping?"[18] with the recession.

There is also the desire of the marketers to continue to sell to the Millennials, especially as these difficult economic times may challenge their spiritual coping skills. Christine Hassler, writing in the *Huffington Post* about women and transformation in this economy, is really hawking her "life coach" services to Millennial women under the heading of 'spiritual transformation.'[19] Her workshop, called Chrysalis, plays on themes of Millennial women as spiritual seekers and promises transformation—the cocoon to butterfly metaphor is taken about as far as one can take such a simplistic image. From the website Chrysalis describes "the delicate process that changes a caterpillar into a beautiful butterfly with intricate and vibrantly colored wings. In this intimate, profound and experiential workshop, you will dive into your feminine being, come out of your cocoon of doubt, anxiety, unworthiness, fear and confusion, and emerge as a much stronger and more beautiful woman for it! Are you ready to spread your wings?"[20] At nearly $700 per workshop, this is a pricey way to find a spiritual path in a severe economic downturn.

Harvard Business School is advising Millennials how to "Recession-Proof Yourself: Four Tips for TwentySomethings." This is another "coach" approach. Eric Chester, President and Founder of Generation Why, Inc. answers the question. According

to the article "Eric works primarily with companies and organiza-
tions that employ teens and young adults. His background as an
invited speaker on career success strategies to more than 1,500
high schools and colleges makes him the perfect coach to field
this question." Work, save, 'shine' and wait for it to be over is the
advice.[21] Chester seems also to be selling his marketing company,
not just sharing his advice.

More disinterested analysts, such as those who write for *The
Economist*, are generally observing that this younger generation
is inclined to step up to the changed work environment without
too much fuss.[22] The Los Angeles Times said basically the same
thing, just with more fanfare. "Are the Millennials the new GI
Generation? Like their great-grandparents, they're entering the
workplace at a time of economic crisis. And they're demonstrating remarkable resilience and optimism."[23] Good news.

But when it comes down to choices between economic neces-
sity and living green, it is "green" that is taking the hit. "Younger
Generation Passes on 'Green' to Save Cash," observes the
Environmental Leader. They report a survey of Millennials on the
green movement and report that "Though conventional wisdom
suggests that the Millennial Generation (ages 13–29) is leading
the charge to make Earth a better place, a survey from Generate
Insight finds that despite being the most environmentally educated, younger members of this generation…71 percent of teens
(ages 13–17) surveyed say if they had to choose between a less
expensive product or one that 'gave back' to the environment,
they would choose the less expensive product."[24]

This suggests that the trailing end of the Millennial Generation
is even more sobered by the economy than the twentysomethings
who have been green for a longer time. The long-term effects of
what appears to be a severe economic downturn and a lagging

jobs rate for years to come may slow or even reverse the green commitment of this younger group.

Digitally innovative, practical, engaged with trying to make the world a better place, still green and spiritual but not religious—that is the Millennial Generation. In 2000, Howe and Strauss, in their generations study of this demographic, *Millennials Rising: The Next Great Generation*, actually came close to predicting the influence of the first completely digital Generation on an election that was eight years in the future. "Over the next decade, the Millennial Generation will entirely recast the image of youth from downbeat and alienated to upbeat and engaged—with potentially seismic consequences for America."[25] Unlike most futuring, this prediction came true in an astonishingly accurate way.

Now many Millennials also have to cope with the difference between their vision for a better world and the realities of their chosen candidate for President, Barack Obama, governing, choosing and being limited by electoral politics. Many representatives of their generation work at very high levels in the new administration. President Obama's chief speechwriter, Jon Favreau, is 27 years old and apparently wrote some of the president's Inaugural Address on a laptop at a Starbucks.[26]

That speech itself was a signal from the Millennial Generation that while campaigning was poetry, governing was not only going to be in prose, it was going to be in an abruptly practical vein. The theme of the much-anticipated Obama Inaugural Address could be summed up as, 'Oh, grow up.' It was a solemn rejection of the myth of American innocence and a signal to this nation that it could no longer afford not to be an adult.

It is astonishing that this speech was written in large part by someone who is not yet thirty years of age. The Inaugural message was based on Paul's First Letter to the Corinthians. "We remain a young nation, but in the words of Scripture, the time has come to set aside childish things."

Time to grow up, America. On January 20, 2009, the Millennial Generation and its new president was telling us this is *not* a time for lofty phrases, but for the solid values that have been forgotten in the years of dangerous innocence in the greed on Wall Street and the bullying practices of our foreign policy.

The majority of the speech, building on this theme of "time to grow up, America," is anything but subtle. Scarcely 150 words into the address and already the president was into the problems that must be faced and the childish mucking about that had gotten us to this pass, especially on the economy. "Our economy is badly weakened, a consequence of greed and irresponsibility on the part of some, but also our collective failure to make hard choices and prepare the nation for a new age."

The Pauline text contains the caution that even adults can't know everything. "For now we see in a mirror dimly, but then face to face." It has been the "know-it-all" attitude of the previous administration that has caused so much damage, especially in foreign policy. This arrogance has led to a disrespect of the rule of law—the way in which undisciplined children will break cherished heirlooms when they storm around in a tantrum. Innocence even in children is not always innocent.

Real grownups take responsibility The challenges are new and the means to solve them may be new, but the values that can carry us there are old: "honesty and hard work, courage and fair play, tolerance and curiosity, loyalty and patriotism—these things are old." Those are the values that mark a mature adult.

The simplicity and strength of the Pauline theme that "the time has come to put away childish things" was the backbone of this address. That it was written by a 27-year-old on a laptop in coffee shop tells you most everything we need to know about the Millennial Generation. They truly have some great moments and the Pauline text is one of them.

The Inaugural address and its strong theme of maturity as a spiritual route for the country contrasts sharply with the theme of butterflies and cocoons. The latter is a cheap and superficial way to think about how spirituality can transform your life. A smattering of Zen Buddhism, Zombism, and digital cowboy narratives aren't going to get you through the hard times for very long. The major religious traditions, when explored deeply and thoroughly, can sustain spirituality for Millennials.

Millennials do not dream of Eden, but religious institutions have failed them in a huge way by not helping them interpret their digital lives in a deeper and more profound story and connecting that story to the largest human story—perhaps we can build on the Inaugural address and its theme of an America less childishly innocent and more mature and awake to its responsibilities.

WISDOM LESSONS FROM
THE "FALL"

A wrecking ball careens toward the word "if," then proceeds to shatter and construct a city from the pieces. A beautiful girl kisses the word "if" then turns into a frog. A young boy waters a beanstalk, the beanstalk shoots up to the sky, a giant climbs down and steps on the boy.[1] What is the message? Imagination is a tricky business.

These are some of the SyFy (formerly SciFi) channel's branded "if" segments, lodged between commercials and programming. These little blips, called "bumpers," jolt the viewer and deliver powerful messages about the unexpected and even dangerous aspects of human imagination in the digital age. These "if" bumpers reveal that innocence in the digital age can turn someone into a frog, or possibly result in death.

These Syfy shorts are little shoots of wisdom spiking up in digital media like science fiction itself, for which the Syfy channel was created. The "if" bumpers are deliberately "weird" in order to show us that the world itself is really pretty weird if only we dare look. But they represent a particularly "wired" kind of wisdom, because the digital age, with its use of rapid images, can end up giving us information in ways that are disconnected and even fragmented. Several times, these "if" bumpers deliberately show images from children's stories such as *The Princess and the Frog*,

or *Jack and the Beanstalk*, to evoke a picture of innocence. Then
the unexpected happens, and the innocent image gets smashed or
changed in a fundamental way. The "if" bumpers signal one of
the ways in which the wired world itself is not innocent; children
must be monitored when they access the Internet because there
are many dangerous images available through their computers,
and there are many dangerous people trying to prey on a child's
innocence through the Internet. Innocence is at greater risk in a
wired world, and the desire for knowledge can lead to some very
terrible things. Yet some of the images, such as the "if" segments,
try to teach us that. The wired world itself sometimes tries to teach
us that innocence is becoming ever more dangerous.

The image of the bitten apple on Apple computers shows us
that the age of computers is not innocent. Through the Internet
we find greater knowledge of good, but also of evil. In a sense, it's
the "Fall" of Adam and Eve from the innocence of the Garden of
Eden all over again, because of the vast amount of new knowledge
available to us through the Internet, and also the vast new ways in
which people can exploit and even harm one another.

Sometimes, however, the power of digital images can be used
for good. Digital images can be put together to show us things
we'd rather not see, and force us to make connections we'd rather
not make about what's wrong in the world, and what needs to be
changed. Our desire for knowledge lures us into this wired world;
it can harm us, or it can help us come to terms with violations of
innocence that must not be allowed to continue. This can take
place in a particularly wired way as happens in the making of
the video, *Jack Bauer Interrogates Santa Claus*[2] created by the
"Rebels Viral Team." Segments of *24* are re-edited with new foot-
age of Santa being tortured by Bauer. Through this media manipulation, Jack Bauer is forced to see himself, and his rogue torture

methods. Splicing clips from the actual program *24* and film of an actor playing Santa Claus into a viral mash up, the video achieves a high level of integration and drama.

In the beginning, Bauer comes into an interrogation room and glares at the video camera on the wall. Santa Claus is tied to a chair and he has been beaten. He has a bleeding cut on his face and blood on his shirt. Jack is carrying a list of names with "naughty" written above one column, and "nice" above the other. Jack places the list on the table in front of Santa. "What are you doing in this country?" he hisses. "Delivering packages," Santa says. "Look," says Santa desperately, "I know how it looks. The beard, the packages, and flying without a passport. But I'm Santa." "Yeah," Jack says, "Prove it!" "Red suit, ringing bells..." Santa protests. "Give me the names!" "Dasher, Dancer, Prancer, Vixen..."

Jack becomes enraged when he gets the truth from Santa. "I'm done talking with you." He whips out a knife, and brandishing it in front of Santa's face, Jack yells, "First, I'll take out your right eye; then when I'm done, I'll move over and take out your left eye, and then I'm going to keep cutting until I get the information I need." But Santa doesn't flinch. "Think about what you're doing, Jack," Santa says. "No present for you this year." Jack backs up. "I don't believe you. You don't understand a thing about me." Jack starts to sweat. "You're on my naughty list now, Jack. The naughty list." Bauer backs away. "You son-of-a-bitch," he says. "Oh, and Jack..." Santa pauses. "Merry Christmas." The last scene shows Jack Bauer weeping with remorse.

The digital age can sometimes provoke us to leap imaginatively over the well-worn divisions of the innocence-versus-guilt version of the Garden of Eden. It can provoke conflicts of conscience over torture. But the wired world doesn't solve these problems and there is still a lot of power in the temptation to be innocent and to escape from all these conflicts and problems. From innocent search engines to a 3-D Garden of Eden, complete with a tree of the knowledge of good and evil, our wired world continues to cycle and recycle the longing for innocence, and the desire to solve the problems of our world by escaping to another. Because of the power of the Internet, longing for innocence can become a business model or a blockbuster movie.

INNOCENT SEARCH ENGINES

'Don't be evil' is the informal corporate motto of Google, the worldwide search engine. Google's brand of not being evil means not only giving first class service to their users, but, actually not being "evil" in their business practices. As their corporate website says, "You can make money without doing evil." Not being evil is good service, but it is also, in Google's terms, behaving ethically as a company. "Yes, it's about providing our users unbiased access to information, focusing on their needs and giving them the best products and services that we can. But it's also about doing the right thing more generally—following the law, acting honorably and treating each other with respect."

Can a huge corporate enterprise such as Google live up to this motto to always be innocent and never engage in "evil"? You take on a boat-load of unrealizable expectations when your corporate brand is based on not being evil. Giant Google bumped into the reality that it actually couldn't conduct business in the Garden of Eden when it decided to do business in China and allow its search results to be censored.

The blogs, of course, went after Google for this hypocrisy and the 'not be evil' brand provoked blogger cynicism. This one is typical, "Online search engine leader Google, Inc. has agreed to censor its results in China, adhering to the country's free-speech restrictions in return for better access in the Internet's fastest growing market. What was that motto again Google? 'Do no evil…' or something like that?"[3] In fact, censorship by Google in various countries had been going on for a while. *Wikipedia* has a whole article on censorship by Google.[4]

But then, Google was hit by cyber-attacks in China. Google maintained on its own blog that "we have evidence to suggest that a primary goal of the attackers was accessing the Gmail accounts of Chinese human rights activists."[5] Google is not the only company that has been cyber-attacked, but it responded by saying it is no longer willing to censor search results on its Chinese servers. Google acknowledged that this decision "may well mean" the closure of Google.cn, the Google site in China. Human Rights Watch praised the decision and urged other firms to follow suit in challenging censorship.

Google climbed back up onto its white horse and said it was sharing the information about the cyber-attacks and the decision not to censor in China anymore, "because this information goes to the heart of a much bigger global debate about freedom of speech." But Evgeny Morozov, an expert on the political effects of the Internet and a Yahoo fellow at Georgetown University, questioned why Google had made the decision after four years. "They knew pretty well what they were getting into. *Now it seems they are playing the innocence card.…* It's like they thought they were dealing with the government of Switzerland and suddenly realized it was China," he said.[6]

"Playing the innocence card" is right. Google saw a chance to get its innocence back in terms of branding, and took it. But some analysts looked deeper, to see if Google's business in China was running at a loss, and that was why they were willing to consider pulling out. Bloggers nailed Google for more hypocrisy. In a post called "China's Google Stance: More About Business Than Thwarting Evil," Sarah Lacey on *TechCrunch* argued that, "1. Google's business was not doing well in China" and "2. Google is ready to burn bridges." Google doesn't have the top market share in China, she argued, and it never was going to have. Instead, "Google has clearly decided doing business in China isn't worth it, and are turning what would be a negative into a marketing positive for its business in the rest of the world." In other words, Google could stop being "evil" by ending censorship in China, supporting human rights activists, and getting kicked out rather than just leaving. If Google had wanted to stay, she continues, they would have worked behind the scenes with the Chinese government. Lecturing the Chinese on Human Rights in an English-language blog is not a good negotiating stance if you want to change things. So Google's just going to throw Chinese Google users "under the bus."[7]

Ditch the motto, Google. That's your problem. You have a Garden of Eden motto in the real world and it doesn't let you make decent business decisions, either how to work with other countries on human rights, or how to bring the Internet to people in countries that are in conflict over censorship. Instead, Google decided to take back it's 'don't be evil' brand by kicking its Chinese customers offline. That's naughty, not nice, Google.

AVATAR

The Garden of Eden film for the I Generation (those born after 1990) is *Avatar*. These are not just digital young people, they're wired. Children in this generation had cell phones as young as four, and by seven have iPods, earpieces, and are online for hours every day, surfing, playing games, and chatting. These young people grew up never knowing a world that wasn't wired. Even if they were born into a family whose parents cannot afford this technology, they see it on television, not only in advertising but also in shows and films.

Video game players know what an avatar is. An avatar is a computer representation of yourself—this can be the three-dimensional kind that game players use, a picture of yourself, or your Internet username. People can choose their own avatars and personalize them as they wish. You can be taller, shorter, younger, older, and you don't particularly even have to be human. Animal avatars are very popular.

Avatar (2009), currently the highest-grossing film of all time, having earned more than 2 billion dollars worldwide and counting, uses both computer generated actors and real actors. James Cameron who wrote, produced, and directed the film delayed production to allow technology to catch up.

The action takes place 200 years in the future on a planet where the evil RDA Corporation is mining for the elusive mineral "unobtainium." They employ mercenaries to protect them. The planet, called "Pandora," is inhabited by the Na'vi who are ten feet tall, blue-skinned, human-looking creatures who live in harmony with nature and worship a mother goddess called Eywa. The Na'vi live near a huge tree they call "hometree" and the mother goddess communicates with them through the tribe's "tree of voices."

The planet's atmosphere is toxic to humans, so scientists have grown biologically identical Na'vi bodies that can be inhabited by genetically matched humans. In a 2007 interview with *Time* magazine, Cameron was asked about the film's name, *Avatar*, and what the implications were that humans could actually physically become their computer avatars. According to Cameron, it means "that the human technology in the future is capable of injecting a human's intelligence into a remotely located body, a biological body."[8]

The hero of the film is a paraplegic former Marine, named Jake. He replaces his twin brother, a scientist, on the project when his brother is killed. The head of military operations, Colonel Miles Quaritch, promises Jake that he will be given new legs to replace his paralyzed ones if he spies on the program and secretly reports to him.

Like *Dances with Wolves*, which it closely resembles, Jake falls in love with the Na'vi culture—its innocence, its beauty and its lovely inhabitant, Neytiri. Jake switches sides and helps the Na'vi warriors defeat the evil corporation and its mercenaries before they can destroy the "tree of souls". Then Jake becomes a real Na'vi through a clan ritual and takes over leadership of the tribe. This is every white, western colonialist fantasy: you can become one of the spiritually adept, native people whom you were formerly trying to kill, you can meet a great girl, teach the primitives how to fight and then they'll make you their leader. What's not to like in that fantasy?

At Comic Con 2009, Cameron told the audience that "the Na'vi represent something that is our higher selves, or our aspirational selves, what we would like to think we are and even though there are good humans in the film, humans represent what we know to be the parts of ourselves that are trashing our world and maybe condemning ourselves to a grim future."[9] In other words, the Na'vi are the innocent Abel to our guilty fallen Cain.

But here's the good news, according to the movie *Avatar*. You can hook up with your innocent self through computer technology.

One of the most fascinating devices in the film is the long braid, like a fiber optic cable, that the Na'vi wear and that they use to "hook up" with the powerful flying predators that they bond with for life and which they use to fly. The braid tail, the computer cord, if you will, is also apparently the way the Na'vi make love. When Jake in his avatar form and Neytiri mate, they "hook up" with their braids. This is very similar to Neo's socket in his head from the *Matrix*, but it is more intimate, with explicit sexual connotations. You can get closer, even closer than your ear buds with your iPhone; a lot closer.

These computer-generated themes of connecting with your innocence through technology are the desire of the Internet generation to overcome their alienation, solve the global climate crisis, and live in harmony with their planet. It's not a bad dream, but it is a dream. Cameron taps into that desire and the Internet generation flocked to see the film, often multiple times. But it is not just the young, Internet generation who long for this kind of 'hooking up' with the spiritual innocence *Avatar* promises.

Older spiritual progressives, like Rabbi Arthur Waskow, explicitly see in *Avatar* the promise of the return to the innocence of the Garden of Eden. At the same time, Waskow singularly fails to grasp the religious and political conflicts of the film, accepting a good/evil dualism as an agenda for both worship and climate change action. As much as I appreciate the dedication of Rabbi Arthur Waskow to peace and justice his hymn of praise to the film *Avatar*, for example, falls into the dangerous innocence category. He sees the "seeds of rebirth" in the movie, even while he condemns the "robotic Marine generals and corporate exploiters of *Avatar* [who] would like to kill Pandora and its God/dess Eywa." Waskow urges that "Jews, Christians, Muslims, Hindus, Buddhists, Wiccans, those who celebrate Manitou/GreatSpirit in the varied forms of Native practice, join for Tu B'Shvat [Jewish holiday celebrating fruit trees] to celebrate the Sacred Forests of our planet."[10]

That is, let's get back to the Garden of Eden. According to the Reformed Jewish online group Aish.com,[11] "Tu B'Shvat, the holiday of fruit trees, recalls the Garden of Eden and the human quest for spiritual refinement."[12] Waskow urges that multi-faith groups should see the film *Avatar* and then join in the Jewish holiday to make 'seeing' the film into "the profound life that 'seeing' God, life and each other that the film calls for."[13]

Unfortunately, however, the price for this return to innocence is a continuation of the colonialist fantasy that white, western people (especially males) can enter into native culture, and also becomes its saviors. For someone as attuned to militarism and racism as Waskow, this oversight is striking. The lure of the dream of innocence in oneness with nature and native culture is more powerful, it seems, than these other, more sinister connotations of the film.

ACHIEVING WISDOM IN A WIRED WORLD

The three themes of this book are war, the economy, and the environment. It is possible to achieve some genuine change if we understand the big lesson of public theology: people are afraid and they want to escape to the safety of innocence. To help people engage the world as it is, and not as they wish it to be, therefore, the role of public theology is to help us find and use emotionally laden, wisdom images that can "go viral" because of the multiplication effect of the digital age. The best images for this task are those that let us see the complexities of creation and destruction and yet not frighten us into running away to a fantasy world of innocence.

Below are three examples of how this can and is happening, and cautionary tales about what happens when we don't get the religious power of making meaning in a wired world.

The Environment: Where the Weird Things Happen

The entire environmental movement is losing ground in public opinion. Some would fault the "Climategate" hacking of emails from climate change scientists in England and the United States In the emails, scientists appear to be conspiring to muzzle critics and bury some research that did not agree with their findings. The scientists clearly also feel embattled by the climate change deniers, but their defensiveness in the stolen emails comes across as untrustworthiness.[14] Others fault the projections or models that scientists use to predict future climate changes and the impacts.

The problem with the public's perception of environmental impacts, however, is that the emotional case has not been made in the public mind. Al Gore's slide shows and lengthy climate change studies like that of the U.N.-sponsored Intergovernmental Panel on Climate Change, don't compel—they preach the same kind of 'goodness' that the *Goode Family* TV show lampooned. The geek-speak and the data-laden studies don't generate any wisdom for people about 'what the heck is happening to me?' And if it isn't about me, it isn't happening—that's one of the lessons of the fall from the Garden of Eden.

The winter of 2010 was the 'snow from hell' year in the United States, particularly in the east and south. There were a couple of weeks when there was snow everywhere except Hawaii. Weird weather disrupted the winter Olympics in Canada, as it alternately rained and then snowed heavily. "Global warming" is a complete failure as the primary description for what is happening to the planet through climate change. It doesn't compute for people, especially when they are digging out from under fifty inches of snow. It doesn't feel like global warming, but it sure is weird.

The world's weather is changing, and changing in dramatic and erratic ways. Hunter Lovins, the cofounder of the Colorado-based Rocky Mountain Institute, is credited with creating the term "global weirding" as a much more descriptive term for what is happening to *us* and what it actually feels like to the average individual. You may not know the cause, but the weather sure has gotten weird.

Thomas Friedman in his book *Hot, Flat and Crowded: Why We Need a Green Revolution—and How it Can Renew America*,[15] likes the Lovins term far better. It's weird and we're saying it's weird. A rise in the "average global temperature is going to lead to all sorts of crazy things—from hotter heat spells and droughts in some places, to colder cold spells and more violent storms, more intense flooding, forest fires and species loss in other places."[16] That does sound a lot like the winter of 2010, what came to be called "snowmageddon" in the media.

Why so much snow? Why is the weather so weird? Well, in the last decades there has been a 4–5 percent increase in the amount of moisture in the atmosphere on the planet due to the warming of the oceans. This extra moisture hits winter weather cold enough to make snow and there you have it, "snowmageddon" measured in feet, not inches, right in the nation's capitol. But like at the Olympics, when the extra moisture met temperatures too warm for snow, it rained. It's not hard to understand, really, but it sure is weird. Kind of feels like the end of the world, doesn't it, when the weather starts being that weird?

I wrote about "global weirding" and "snowmageddon" for the *Washington Post*'s "On Faith" blog. I argued that we need to give up on the nice-sounding, gentle-seeming, bathing-suit wearing weather kind of language that "global warming" implies, and get to the weirdness of it all. I also wrote about the "sin" of climate change deniers, digging out from under this weird, weird weather and still refusing to connect the dots on climate change.[17]

"Pathetically Incorrect!" railed the conservative blogs, specifically about what I had written.[18] "Global Warming Snow Job" bellowed the right-leaning *Washington Times*.[19] "Global weirding" hits a conservative nerve in the way that "global warming" never has and never will. Every time the weather is not sweltering, the climate change denier will find it easy to connect with people's personal experience of the weather. It's not warm, hence, no global warming.

But weird is something else altogether. Weird names the scary, weird is what's happening to me, weird is disorderly and chaotic and *not innocent at all*. Global weirding is climate wisdom in a wired world because it cannot be rationally dismissed or denied. You feel it, you get it, and you get a clue. Wired wisdom needs to get around the rationalistic defenses people throw up against information they don't really want to hear and that they feel they can't do anything about. But weird? I can relate to that. I can feel that, and suddenly my rationalistic defenses are by-passed and there you are—a little wiser about the planet and the changes that are happening. You can run from innocence, but you sure as heck have a harder time running from the connections that happen when your emotions get engaged.

Environmentalists need to get out of the Garden of Eden and get into the real world where the weird things happening.

A Picture Is Worth a Thousand Words

President Obama's salute to the soldiers killed in Afghanistan as their remains were returned to Dover Air Force base should have become the administration's wired message on war.[20] This one picture signaled a different understanding of war that was emerging from the administration. Unfortunately, and this is deeply unfortunate, the lesson about the profound capacity of the wired world to help make a defining image of this nation, this president, and war, has not been learned. This one symbol of the salute could have become a point of emotional connection between the deeply religious Obama and a deeply religious American public. The picture asks, "Is war a bloodless and mindless kind of Nintendo game, or is it a bloody and costly sacrifice?"

Instead of following up on the power of this one image to speak volumes about the president and war, and trying to make the image "go viral" by circulating it on the web, the administration turned to speeches to convey this message. Words have a place in leadership, but they do not convey the depth of wisdom as did the photos of a midnight trip to Dover, and hours of standing in the dark and cold. This picture was made possible because of the changed policy on allowing photos of the return of the war dead when families permit it. That changed policy was part of the new understanding of war emerging from this administration. The policy in action said that war is extremely costly and never innocent. But the insight and the moment were largely wasted even though moving speeches on war as sacrifice followed.

Not long after the Dover salute, at Arlington National Cemetery, President Obama said, "In this time of war, we gather here mindful that the generation serving today already deserves a place alongside previous generations for the courage they have shown and the sacrifices they have made.[21] Later that week, at Elmendorf Air Force Base, on his way to Asia, the president told the assembled troops that that knew "with service comes sacrifice."[22] At the Fort Hood memorial service, the president made the connection himself—he repudiated the idea of war as divinely authorized triumph, and explicitly invoked Lincoln: "And instead of claiming God for our side, we remember Lincoln's words, and always pray to be on the side of God."[23]

But we have to remember that Lincoln did not live in a wired world. Neither did Eisenhower. World War II was a "good war" against a clearly evil axis that attacked without provocation, committed genocide, and sexually enslaved women. It was also a war of national sacrifice. The photos from World War II often depicted heroism. For example, the powerful image of raising the flag at Iwo Jima was actually not the first, but the second flag raising there, and controversy arose over whether it was staged. Nonetheless, this photo has been reproduced many times, and is the basis for a statue that stands at Arlington. This photo typifies the idea that war is about heroic action.

During the Vietnam War, by contrast, the nightly news showed photos of "body bags" being unloaded, week after week, and this changed Americans' perceptions of that war. The Vietnam War took place at the beginning of the electronic media age. The photos from this era, relentlessly showing the carnage of the loss of American lives, challenged the heroic speeches coming out of Washington, both in the Johnson and Nixon administrations. Despite the presidential cheering, Americans *saw* that the war was purposeless and costly. The contrast between body bags and Washington rhetoric about the war destroyed American trust in our goals in that effort.

The Gulf War was called a "Nintendo War" with technological superiority and an explicit connection to the developing video game culture as the wired world took off. Pictures of body bags were outlawed, and many of the photos and fuzzy, black-and-white videos, were taken thousands of feet in the air as the bombs dropped. It's a lot harder to see carnage from the sky.

Then came the war of choice, the Iraq War. "Shock and awe," a phrase right out of the New Testament Book of Revelation, signaled not only a theology of war as earthly triumph, but of heavenly significance as well. It was proposed as an "innocent" war because we were fighting "evil" with "good intentions." The Bush administration tried to censor the images of that war, with national media "embedded" with the troops and thus co-opted in their objective reporting, but, as was noted in Chapter 6, *Comedy Central* became the source of real news about the war, and then the blogsphere took over and the story of the war, and of the torture practiced on prisoners, came out.

American religious and political conservatives are still pushing the dream of war as cosmic triumph despite the fact that both wars they launched and pursued (Iraq and Afghanistan) are national nightmares and have lost considerable support among the American people. The only way for the Obama administration to have changed the script on these stupid and costly wars was, however, to have realized the symbolic power of the image of the salute, and generated the emotional connection to the policy shift around the profound change from war as a "Nintendo game" or a scene out of the Book of Revelation to the reality of war as costly and bloody and deadly sacrifice.

In the war of symbols, this kind of basic struggle for wired wisdom is, as yet, not gaining ground. And we'd better hurry up and wise up about symbols when it comes to war. We're losing on that ground as well.

Zombie Economics: Why Reaganomics
Still Lives

Paul Krugman, the Nobel Prize–winning economist, Princeton Professor, and popular writer, wrote a column titled *All the President's Zombies* during the height of the "summer of hate" (2009) town hall rage over health care. Krugman confessed his depression that the "zombie doctrine" of Reaganism, which says "government intervention is always bad, and leaving the private sector to its own devices is always good" is still so alive in the public mind, when it has been dead and dysfunctional for decades.

According to Krugman, it's the "zombie doctrine" of Reaganomics that killed the economy and brought about the largest economic depression since the Great Depression. "There's a lot to be said about the financial disaster of the last two years, but the short version is simple: politicians in the thrall of Reaganite ideology dismantled the New Deal regulations that had prevented a banking crises for half a century, believing that financial markets could take care of themselves. The effect was to make the financial system vulnerable to a 1930s-style crisis—and the crisis came. 'We have always known that heedless self-interest was bad morals,' said Franklin Delano Roosevelt in 1937. 'We know now that it is bad economics.' And last year we learned that lesson all over again."[24]

So, in short, "it's the zombies, stupid," to paraphrase President Clinton's unofficial campaign slogan when he ran against the first President Bush. Krugman has a gift for communicating in (and I hope he will accept this as praise) "public theology."

The image of undead Reaganomics driving our current politics is almost unparalleled in its clarity and its ability to capture the anxieties of our time as shown in the number of zombies everywhere. Even, apparently, in Congress.

Krugman understands that Ronald Reagan didn't just change our tax code, he "sought to change America's thinking as well." This is something he fears the Obama administration does not understand. People think in images. Remember "morning in America"? These days, in a "wired world," just preaching like Roosevelt against the "bad morals" of selfishness in economics is not going to get regulation back. Compounding the problem is the fact that the banks and insurance companies and the rest are all wired too. That makes their mistakes bigger and faster and it makes them more nimble than the regulators.

This is why we need to learn from "Cain-sian" economics.[25] The worldwide financial system is loaded with human frailty and human creativity. It is a system that is certainly not run by God, but it's not run by the devil either. It's not capitalism per se that's broken, it's the understanding of human nature that used to guide the regulation, or lack of regulation of capitalism that is broken. You cannot take self-interest out of the equation without letting in a horde of risk takers who are rewarded whether the system goes boom or bust. That's just asking for trouble, and trouble is what we've got.

The kind of economic theory that ignores human frailty and argues 'just let the market handle it' has failed over and over again. Yet, as Krugman evokes with his vivid language and gift for imagery, like the undead "zombies," Reaganomics won't lie down and die.

VERIZON: WISER ABOUT SYMBOLS IN
A WIRED WORLD

At the end of the day, religion, all religion, asks two questions: "Am I alone?" and "What can I trust?" Successful politicians know that trust is the key to selling themselves to the public; it's why they so often present themselves as deeply religious. Politicians talking about their religious faith is cultural code for "you can trust me, I believe in God."

This need for trust and connection to others drives culture, and it also drives politics. In the realm of culture, consider the famous Verizon ad and how it captures the viewer's need to be supported in the often-scary world of technology. The fortunate Verizon customer is surrounded by a huge group of support people, while the unfortunate customer who has another cell phone service is virtually alone trying to make contact in cyberspace. The success of this ad campaign is due to the fact that it connects to the fundamental human need, the deeply religious need, to be reassured that 'you are not alone' and it also directly addresses the anxiety and alienation created by technology.

The way to combat the "zombism" of undead Reaganomics is with the same emotional message as the one being peddled by Verizon, 'you are not alone.' By contrast, the conservative public message is that people are "individuals" who stand proudly alone and value freedom and democracy; this is the picture "Tea Party" activists try to project. Anti-government individualism is driving the image market of politics today just as it did in the time of Reagan.

Imagine, however, that instead of the Verizon customer backed up by engineers, programmers, technicians and support people, the image is of a U.S. citizen surrounded by doctors, nurses, teachers, police, highway repair crews, meat inspectors, and on and on. Government is not the enemy, it's the reason we can trust that the meat we eat will not give us food poisoning, it's the ambulance that comes to the rescue when a loved one is having a heart attack, it's having people there who watch out for our safety from terrorists. Being connected to others is a source of protection, comfort, and strength.

People are also afraid of being alone. People fear being isolated; to survive and thrive human beings have families and societies that protect them emotionally, physically, and psychologically. Being alone is a source of threat. The emotional pushback to the threat of being alone is the strong pro-family messaging that conservatives have marketed so well. This is the antidote to the rugged individualism whose unarticulated message is, "you're on your own."

If we begin to think in a "wired" way about how to "change people's thinking" (as Krugman notes Reagan did), we'll immediately see how dispassionate and even weak the alternative usually proposed, the common good, seems. The common good is descriptively correct, but too emotionally distant for people to make a strong connection with it. In addition, it is simply true that powerful messages, especially in our alienated, wired world, have to be about "you." Even family, the marketing people tell us, is secondary for people. In 2006, *Time*'s "Person of the Year" was "You."[26] "You," claimed *Time*, make podcasts, post films on YouTube, participate in MySpace, and create online avatars, and "The tool that makes this possible is the World Wide Web." Today, because of this phenomenon *Time* so correctly identified, we have to tell people "what's in it for you" for any alternative messaging to get traction and be powerful.

Much of the cultural shift toward conservatism over the last few decades has its roots in the turbulent 1960s and the social fragmentation that was unleashed by the Civil Rights movement, the anti-war movement, and the women's movement. Digital messages that say "you are not alone" give us a way to transform the politics of anger that has been so paralyzing for the country for the last four decades, and deal with the warp-speed anxiety of our age.

While we cannot simply appropriate the Verizon ad, we can learn from it. Imagine this YouTube video: a family is driving in their minivan over a bridge; the children are squabbling merrily in the backseat, the dog is shedding, and the parents are talking. The camera pans to the area underneath the bridge and there is an army of people there, legislators, engineers, voters, all of them physically supporting the bridge so the family can drive home in safety. What's the message? "Americans support each other—government, it's all of us." Or, for example, imagine a video of a woman who calls an ambulance because her husband is having a heart attack. We see her arguing with a private ambulance company who responded and demanded cash up front before they would take her husband anywhere. "Where is the county ambulance service?" she asks, aghast. "Smaller government means budget cuts," they reply. "Public services mean you are not alone."

Dangerous innocence cannot be confronted in an abstract way. The wired world, however, gives us many opportunities to generate pictures that deal with fear (bridges that aren't repaired collapse), and also show how values of connection can make a society stronger. This is a message the Millennials and the I-Generation need to learn, and frankly long to hear, and that their parents need to remember. We need the "public theologians" like Krugman to point out the zombies among us, like the undead of Reagaonomics. We need the new populism of the wired generations to connect to the wisdom of Cain and Abel, and the "Fall" from the innocence of the Garden of Eden—human beings can be really destructive, but they have the capacity to be incredibly creative, compassionate, and innovative. We may not always prevent all war, but we grieve it and realize its cost and bring it to an end. The planet's climate is becoming really, really weird right in your driveway, and you have a personal stake in helping change that unless you want to be shoveling even more. At the end of the day, it's all about *you.* Luckily, you are not alone.

"WHAT HATH GOD WROUGHT?"

In 1844 Samuel Morse sent the first public telegram in the United States. His message? "What hath God wrought?" That's the real question, isn't it? What *is* God up to, either in the lines of Morse code as it was first electrically transmitted, or in the lines of computer code that stream around the world today? Is there an electronic age message for us, not just in the words, but in the fact of a wired world itself? That's public theology—a process of discerning what kind of meaning God and human beings are, together, making in this wired world. And not unlike the divine-human relationship since the time of the "Fall" from the Garden of Eden, this relationship is fraught with conflict and possibility, danger, and opportunity. But now it's wired, and our wisdom needs to be wired too.

NOTES

INTRODUCTION

1. http://www.theapplemuseum.com/index.php?id=44/.
2. http://www.vonnegutweb.com/vonnegutia/commencement/syracuse.html/.
3. Throughout this book, liberalism is understood not in the recent "culture wars" definition as positions on certain political issues such as abortion or homosexuality, but in the classical sense of the rise of Enlightenment individualism, faith in human reason, and, in religion, an emphasis on personal experience over transcendent revelation. Progressivism, by contrast, has a more communitarian and working-class background. Re this history of progressivism, see John Podesta, *The Power of Progress: How America's Progressives Can (Once Again) Save Our Economy, Our Climate, and Our Country* (New York: Random House, 2008), Chapter 1.
4. http://latimesblogs.latimes.com/washington/2009/08/obama-joker-artist.html/.
5. Rick Perlstein, *Nixonland: The Rise of a President and the Fracturing of America* (New York: Scribner, 2008), p. 747.
6. Ibid.

CHAPTER 1

1. Susan Brooks Thistlethwaite, "Mel Makes a War Movie," *Chicago Tribune* (February 23, 2003). See also, Susan Brooks Thistlethwaite, "Mel Makes a War Move," *in Perspectives on the Passion of the Christ: Religious Thinkers and Writers Explore the Issues Raised by the Controversial Movie* (New York: Hyperion, 2004).
2. David Van Biema et al., "Why Did Jesus Die?" *Time* (April 12, 2004), 60. http://www.time.com/time/magazine/article/0,9171,993793,00.html/.
3. Chris Hedges, *American Fascists: The Christian Right and the War on America* (New York: Free Press, 2006), 10–36.
4. http://www.apwu.org/join/women/lbportraits/portraits-labor-triangle.htm/.
5. Ibid, "Sweatshop exploitation still exists. Studies by the Labor Department in the mid-1990s found that 67 percent of garment factories in Los Angeles and 63 percent of those in New York violate minimum wage and overtime laws. Even worse, the study found that 98 percent of Los Angeles' garment factories have workplace health and safety problems that could cause injuries or death."

CHAPTER 2

1. Thomas L. Friedman, The World Is Flat: A Brief History of the Twenty-first Century (New York: Farrar, Straus and Giroux, 2005).
2. See Douglas Coupland's official website for books, his blog, and other essays. http://www.coupland.com/.
3. See Dennis Overbye, "They Tried to Outsmart Wall Street," The New York Times (March 9, 2009) http://www.nytimes.com/2009/03/10/science/10quant. html?pagewanted=2&_r=1. It is revealing that this critique of the theory behind derivatives is in the science section of the NYT.
4. This point will be further developed in the conclusion.
5. http://www.hrtechnews.com/tag/blackberry/.
6. Reinhold Niebuhr, The Nature and Destiny of Man: Volume I: Human Nature (Louisville, KY: Westminster John Knox Press, 1996), p. 178. Originally published by Charles Scribner's Sons, 1941.
7. Ibid, p. 191.
8. In the extraordinary five-volume series called the "Fundamentalism Project," world historian William McNeill sums up the relationship between fundamentalism and the dislocations of the modern world. "The radical instability that prevails worldwide, as the human majority emerges painfully from rural isolation and struggles to accommodate itself to the dictates of an exchange economy, gives religious fundamentalists an extraordinary opportunity to channel mass responses either into an angry assault on aliens and infidels or toward peaceable symbiosis with strangers."

CHAPTER 3

1. John Mickelthwait and Adrian Wooldrige, God Is Back: How the Global Revival of Faith is Changing the World (New York: Penguin Press, 2009).
2. Nightline, 3/4/04, NO30304-01.
3. Ron Suskind, The Way of the World: A Story of Truth and Hope in an Age of Extremism (New York: HarperCollins, 2008), 10.
4. Ibid, 24.
5. Perlstein, Nixonland, p. 747.
6. Madeleine Albright, The Mighty and the Almighty: Reflections on America, God and World Affairs (New York: Harper Collins, 2006).
7. http://en.wikipedia.org/wiki/Jerry_Falwell/.
8. Fareed Zakaria, "The Politics of Rage: Why Do They Hate Us?" http://www.fareedzakaria.com/ARTICLES/newsweek/101501_why.html/.
9. Fox News reporting well captured the themes of good versus evil in President Bush's speech at the Statue of Liberty one year after the 9/11 attacks. http://www.foxnews.com/story/0,2933,62716,00.html/.
10. Woodward, Plan, p. 379.
11. Thomas E. Ricks, Fiasco: The American Military Adventure in Iraq (New York: Penguin Press, 2006).
12. Ibid, 16.
13. http://middleeast.about.com/od/iraq/ig/Abu-Ghraib-Torture-Photos/Inhuman-pyramid-at-Abu-Ghraib.html/.
14. Mayer, pp. 118–119.

15. Ibid, p. 174.
16. http://pewforum.org/docs/?DocID=156/.
17. http://cbs13.com/watercooler/Churgoers.torture.pew.2.1000890.html/.
18. http://www.ap-gfkpoll.com/pdf/AP-GfK_Poll_Supreme_Court_Final_ Topline.pdf/.
19. http://www.thenation.com/blogs/notion/157437/.
20. http://www.mcclatchydc.com/2010/02/19/86581/no-penalty-recommended-for-lawyers.html/.

CHAPTER 4

1. http://www.newsweek.com/id/100454/.
2. *The Colbert Report,* http://www.colbertnation.com/the-colbert-report-videos/210798/november-19-2008/the-word—mad-men/.
3. Robert J. Shiller, "Infectious Exuberance," http://www.theatlantic.com/doc/print/200807/housing?x=43&y=4/.
4. Cf. http://www.law.cornell.edu/uscode/html/uscode12/usc_sec_12_00001828—-000-.html 1828. (a)(1)(b)/. "Each sign required under subparagraph (A) shall include a statement that insured deposits are backed by the full faith and credit of the United States Government."
5. http://www.pbs.org/newshour/businessdesk/2008/11/do-you-think-alan-greenspan-re.html/.
6. Ibid.
7. Paul Muolo and Mathew Padilla, *Chain of Blame: How Wall Street Caused the Mortgage and Credit Crisis* (Hoboken, NJ: John Wiley and Sons, 2008), p. 291.
8. http://www.youtube.com/watch?v=1RZVw3no2A4&annotation_id=annotation_918789&feature=iv/.
9. Muolo and Padilla, *Chain of Blame.*
10. Tim LaHay et al., *Left Behind.*
11. Before joining *CNBC*, Santelli worked at the Institutional Financial Futures and Options at Sanwa Futures (in the area of institutional trading and hedge funds). Before that, he worked as managing director at the Derivative Products Group of Geldermann, Inc. The derivatives, the bundles of bad debt sold off at enormous profits, is one of the biggest engines of the financial meltdown.
12. http://www.eschatonblog.com/.
13. http://mortgage.freedomblogging.com/2008/12/01/popular-mortgage-blogger-and-stinging-media-critic-dies-at-47/.
14. Ibid.
15. Ibid.
16. Muolo and Padilla, *Chain of Blame,* p. 305.
17. http://www.businessinsider.com/the-next-housing-bubble-is-here-2009-10/.

CHAPTER 5

1. http://www.quotesdaddy.com/author/Ken+Ham/.
2. http://www.answersingenesis.org/articles/wow/evolutionizing-culture/.

3. http://www.answersincreation.org/.
4. See http://www.pamd.uscourts.gov/kitzmiller/04cv2688-111.pdf/.
5. Thomas Frank, *What's the Matter with Kansas? How Conservatives Won the Heart of America* (New York: Henry Holt, 2004), p. 247.
6. Ibid, p. 207. See also www.answersingenesis.org/.
7. One of the leaders of the Human Genome Project, however, is Francis Collins, a Christian evangelical who rejects ideas of intelligent design, but supports a role for God in evolution.
8. http://hea.sagepub.com/cgi/content/short/6/4/445/.
9. http://christiansandclimate.org/learn/call-to-action/.
10. Ibid, p. 1.
11. Ibid, p. 2.
12. Ibid.
13. Ibid, p. 3.
14. http://www.citizenlink.org/pdfs/NAELetterFinal.pdf/.
15. Bill Moyers, "Is God Green?" http://www.pbs.org/moyers/moyersonamerica/green/index.html/.
16. http://www.christianitytoday.com/ct/2008/decemberweb-only/150-41.0.html/.
17. http://www.earthfirst.org/about.htm/.
18. Al Gore, *An Inconvenient Truth: The Planetary Emergency of Global Warming and What We Can Do About It* (New York: Rodale, 2006), p. 12.
19. Ibid.
20. George Will, "Green with Guilt about Planet-Saving," *Chicago Tribune* (June 5, 2009).

CHAPTER 6

1. Glen Stassen, ed., *Just Peacemaking: The New Paradigm for Ethics of Peace and War* (Cleveland, OH: Pilgrim Press, 2008).
2. http://newsweek.washingtonpost.com/onfaith/panelists/susan_brooks_thistlethwaite/2009/12/just_war_and_just_peace_the_emerging_obama_doctrine.html (Italics added).
3. http://www.usip.org/pubs/specialreports/sr214.html/.
4. "Self-consciousness means the recognition of finiteness within infinity" (Niebuhr, *Moral Man and Immoral Society,* p. 42).
5. Ellen Warren, "Chris Rock: Forever in a Hard Place," *Chicago Tribune* (October 4, 2009), Section 4, p. 4.
6. http://www.thedailyshow.com/video/index.jhtml?videoId=217705/.
7. http://www.usatoday.com/tech/science/2007-03-27-maya-2012_n.htm/.
8. http://www.nytimes.com/2010/01/08/arts/television/08simpsons.html?pagewanted=print/.
9. Henry R. Luce, "The American Century" reprinted in *The Ambiguous Legacy*, ed. M. J. Hogan (Cambridge: Cambridge University Press, 1999).
10. Perlstein, *Nixonland*, p. 99.
11. Ibid, p. 102.
12. Ibid.
13. Stanley Karnow, *Viet Nam: A History* (New York: Viking Press, 1983), p. 336.

CHAPTER 7

1. http://www.msnbc.msn.com/id/26315908/#30079184/.
2. Ibid.
3. http://www.nea.fr/html/law/nlb/Nlb-62/sandslov.pdf/.
4. http://www.gwu.edu/~nsarchiv/NSAEBB/NSAEBB195/index.htm/.
5. *Physics in the Contemporary World*, Arthur D. Little Memorial Lecture at MIT (November 25, 1947).
6. http://www.jkrowling.com/.
7. See chapter 9.
8. http://www.esiweb.org/enlargement/?cat=81#awp::?cat=81/.
9. http://www.youtube.com/watch?v=PNQQyKBml04/, see also, http://foreign.senate.gov/testimony/2009/ClintonTestimony090113a.pdf/.
10. Clifford Geertz, *The Interpretation of Cultures* (New York: Basic Books, 1975).
11. http://www.whitehouse.gov/the_press_office/Remarks-by-the-President-at-Cairo-University-6-04-09/.
12. Mickelthwait and Wooldrige, *God Is Back*.

CHAPTER 8

1. http://www.wikiality.com/Moneytheism/.
2. James P. Pinkerton, "As Rove Moves On, It's Back to the Future," *Newsday* (August 14, 2007).
3. "Efficient Market Hypothesis," www.wikipedia.org/.
4. http://newsweek.washingtonpost.com/onfaith/panelists/susan_brooks_thistlethwaite/2008/10/warren_buffett_american_dumble.html/.
5. Kevin Phillips, *Bad Money: Reckless Finance, Fail* (New York: Viking, 2008), p. 89. http://www.thedailyshow.com/video/index.jhtml?videoId=220538&title=Jim-Cramer-Pt.-2&byDate=trueed Politics, and the Global Crisis of American Capitalism/.
6. Kevin Phillips, *American Theocracy: The Peril and Politics of Radical Religion, Oil, and Borrowed Money in the 21st Century* (New York: Viking, 2006).
7. Ibid, p. 91.
8. http://www.huffingtonpost.com/arianna-huffington/larry-summers-brilliant-m_b_178956.h...3/26/2009/.
9. Thomas Frank, *One Market Under God: Extreme Capitalism, Market Populism, and the End of Economic Democracy* (New York: Random House, 2000), p. 171.
10. Ibid, p. 172.
11. Frank, *What's the Matter with Kansas?*, p. 245.
12. Ibid., p. 2. www.huffingtonpost.com/ariana-huffinton/larry-summers/.
13. The dignity of human beings transcends work, of course. Work is a means by which dignity is exercised. People who cannot work because of handicapping conditions or other problems do not cease having dignity, though a failure to provide adequate care for them also insults their dignity and worth. The key insight of progressivism on human nature, however, is that it is fundamentally

dynamic rather than static. Economic systems are most robust when human beings are the active subjects, not the passive objects of these systems.

14. Niebuhr, *Moral Man and Immoral Society*.
15. Adam Smith, *An Inquiry into the Nature and Causes of the Wealth of Nations*, reprint (Chicago: University of Chicago Press, 1976), pp. 26–27, cited in Rebecca M. Blank and William McGurn, *Is the Market Moral: A Dialogue on Religion, Economics and Justice* (Washington, DC: Brookings Institution Press, 2004), p. 54.
16. "Three Trillion Dollars Later..." *The Economist* (May 16, 2009), p. 13.

CHAPTER 9

1. http://www.youtube.com/watch?v=-4snMqlkFnM/.
2. The naming of "generations" comes from the work of William Strauss and Neil Howe, whose book *Generations: The History of America's Future, 1584 to 2069* (1991) was influential in starting the generational naming trend. Howe and Strauss maintain that they use the term "Millennials" in place of "Generation Y" because the members of the generation themselves coined the term, not wanting to be associated with Generation X. In 2000, these authors followed up with a book on this new demographic called *Millennials Rising: The Next Great Generation*.
3. http://www.environmentalleader.com/2009/04/23/.
4. http://www.pubmedcentral.nih.gov/articlerender.fcgi?artid=1278473/.
5. Ibid.
6. http://www.pewforum.org/newassets/images/reports/millennials/millennials-report.pdf/, p. 3.
7. Ibid., p. 2.
8. My thanks to Lester Feder for this key insight.
9. http://www.kxan.com/dpp/news/Road_signs_warn_of_zombies/; http://www.youtube.com/watch?v=s6skRzNdJtg/.
10. *Chicago Tribune* (July 9, 2009).
11. Jane Austen and Seth Grahame-Smith, *Pride and Prejudice and Zombies* (Philadelphia, PA: Quirk Books, 2009), pp. 14–15.
12. Steve Prothero, "Is Religion Losing the Millennial Generation?" http://blogs.usatoday.com/oped/2008/02/is-religion-los.html/.
13. "Whassup? A Glimpse Into the Attitudes and Beliefs of the Millennial Generation," http://www.collegevalues.org/seereview.cfm?id=613.
14. "U.S. Religious Landscape Survey," http://religions.pewforum.org/comparisons#/.
15. Ibid., pp. 7–8. "Whassup?"
16. Thus the 2010 Pew study on Millennials finds their religious beliefs "fairly traditional." http://www.pewforum.org/newassets/images/reports/millennials/millennials-report.pdf/, p. 2.
17. Wendy Koop, *One Day, All Children...: The Unlikely Triumph of Teach For America and What I Learned Along the Way* (New York: PublicAffairs, 2003).
18. http://www.ypulse.com/tales-of-a-twentysomething-nothing/.
19. http://www.huffingtonpost.com/christine-hassler/the-rite-of-passage-for-t_b_210095.html/.

20. http://www.christinehassler.com/archived_letter/ChrysalisJuly2009.html/.
21. http://blogs.harvardbusiness.org/goldsmith/2008/11/recessionproof_yourself_four_t.html/.
22. http://www.economist.com/businessfinance/displayStory.cfm?story_id=12863573/.
23. http://www.latimes.com/news/opinion/la-oe-winogradhais21-2009jun21,0,4189888.story/.
24. http://www.environmentalleader.com/2009/04/23/younger-generation-confused-about-green/.
25. Ibid., back cover.
26. http://www.washingtonpost.com/wp-dyn/content/article/2008/12/17/AR2008121703903.html/.

CONCLUSION

1. http://www.youtube.com/watch?v=qvq1q2vgObc/. Thanks to Douglas Thistlethwaite for pointing out these "If" bumpers to me.
2. http://www.rebelchristmascard2009.com/.
3. http://digg.com/tech_news/Google_Agrees_to_Censor_Results_in_China/.
4. http://en.wikipedia.org/wiki/Censorship_by_Google/.
5. http://googleblog.blogspot.com/2010/01/new-approach-to-china.html
6. http://www.guardian.co.uk/technology/2010/jan/12/google-china-ends-censorship (italics added).
7. http://techcrunch.com/2010/01/12/google%E2%80%99s-china-stance-more-about-business-than-thwarting-evil/.
8. Winters Keegan, Rebecca (January 11, 2007). "Q&A with James Cameron," *Time Magazine*. http://www.time.com/time/arts/article/0,8599,1576622,00.html#ixzz0a69HUhNB/.
9. Associated Press (July 24, 2009). "James Cameron wows Comic Con with 3-D 'Avatar'—BostonHerald.com," *News.bostonherald.com*. http://news.bostonherald.com/track/celebrity/view/20090724james_cameron_wows_comic_con_with_3-d_avatar/.
10. http://newsweek.washingtonpost.com/onfaith/panelists/arthur_waskow/2010/01/avatar_film_us_climate_policy_festival_of_trees_rebirthday.html.
11. http://www.aish.com/h/15sh/i/48961111.html.
12. http://www.aish.com/h/15sh/i/48961111.html.
13. Waskow.
14. Global Doubting," *Chicago Tribune* (February 17, 2010), p. 18.
15. http://www.thomaslfriedman.com/bookshelf/hot-flat-and-crowded/.
16. http://www.nytimes.com/2007/12/02/opinion/02friedman.html?_r=1/.
17. http://newsweek.washingtonpost.com/onfaith/panelists/susan_brooks_thistlethwaite/2010/02/got_snow_maybe_its_climate_change.html/.
18. http://eric-graff.blogspot.com/2010/02/global-weirding-its-sin-not-to-be-green.html/.
19. http://www.washingtontimes.com/news/2010/feb/11/global-warming-snow-job/?feat=home_headlines/.
20. http://www.washingtonpost.com/wp-dyn/content/article/2009/10/29/AR2009102904746html/.

21. http://www.whitehouse.gov/the-press-office/remarks-president-veterans-day-arlington-national-cemetery/.
22. http://www.whitehouse.gov/the-press-office/remarks-president-service-members-elmendorf-air-force-base-anchorage-alaska/.
23. http://www.whitehouse.gov/the-press-office/remarks-president-memorial-service-fort-hood/.
24. Paul Krugman, "All the President's Zombies." http://www.nytimes.com/2009/08/24/opinion/24krugman.html?_r=1/.
25. See chapter 8.
26. http://www.time.com/time/magazine/article/0,9171,1569514,00.html/.